"Yet another NEW perspective from the Masters! If there was such a thing as something more than a 360-degree view, Perry and Haluska have invented it. Once again, I am totally amazed at their ability to surgically uncover details, perspectives, viewpoints, and needs in order to satisfy the mission of the employer, the applicant, the Team, and the company! Having partners like these guys is almost an unfair advantage to accelerating success and ultimately the bottom line! I am both anxious and in awe, wondering what else they can come out with! *Prisa!!!*"

– Larry Mench, Vice President of US Operations,
Tim Hortons USA, Inc.

"CEOs consistently rank 'human capital' as one of the most important challenges to the success of their organizations. Addressing that challenge requires hiring great (not simply good) leaders. *Hiring Greatness* provides indispensable insight into exactly what it takes to make that a reality!"

—Timothy Keiningham, *New York Times*
bestselling author of *The Wallet Allocation Rule*

"Just when I thought he said it all, David Perry does it again! He is walking proof that 'creativity' and 'out-of-the-box' thinking will enable success for us all. Having had the pleasure to read all his books, I remain amazed by his informative and innovative approach with each reading, which builds upon prior writings. *Hiring Greatness* introduced a unique formula for recruiting top-notch talent, which I intend to deploy at Numerix. *Hiring Greatness* is thought provoking! It has caused me to re-think my entire approach to hiring C-level candidates, or any potential employee for that matter. Numerix will now seek to locate 'future employees' who are not 'currently running away, but toward something,' as David suggest in *Hiring Greatness*. All hiring managers at any company and in any industry must add *Hiring Greatness* to their reading list."

—Steven R. O'Hanlon, CEO and President, Numerix LLC

"Why would you bother to accept performance that's 'good enough'? Just because it's acceptable, or it passed a litmus test? I don't think so. Since we too often have experienced good we certainly know Great is Better. And you can have Great by HIRING GREAT. David helped me Hire Great, by adding a final member to my team back in 2008. I witnessed these techniques first hand, more than once, and if applied boldly and with fervor, can attest that you too will *HIRE GREATNESS*."

—Rudy Richman, VP, Sales and Marketing,
Privacy Analytics

"The recruiting industry often operates using smoke and mirrors. Misdirection enables many firms to deliver mediocrity. Mr. Perry smashes the mirrors and clears the smoke. In colorful fashion, he has given power back to companies permitting them to extract true value from their recruitment projects and grow their business with top tier executives—difference makers. Also a great read for every executive search professional. David has laid out a brilliant road map for those individuals to become industry leaders."

—Barry Johnston, VP Operations, Ignite Technical Resources

"In today's highly competitive market, companies that want to attract, *and keep*, star players had better understand what makes stars shine. Perry and Haluska challenge the usual—conventional, outmoded, and ultimately, inherently faulty—approaches to hiring the best and provide a clear, step-by-step process to getting it right."

—Nathalie Thompson, author of *fearLESS: How to Conquer Your Fear, Stop Playing Small and Start Living an Extraordinary Life You Love*

"Most Canadians don't use language like how to 'crush' your competition, but they are kidding themselves if they think that tough executives in the US and China aren't thinking of doing that each and every day. In their book *Hiring Greatness*, David Perry and Mark Haluska point out that there is no substitute for hiring the best—it's people after all who produce income not assets. That's the difference between having a CEO like Steve Jobs at Apple or a Mike Zafirovski at Nortel. Some difference. In this amazingly candid, must-read, David and Mark disclose secrets to great recruiting—things like 'never hire a liar,' 'people don't quit companies, they quit bosses,' and 'compensation is far more than just monetary' will take your company to a whole other level."

—Bruce M Firestone, PhD, *Ottawa Senators founder*

"We are advocates for advancing Canada as a competitive innovation nation where our firms stay ahead of global competition. The way to do this is to excel at strategy, talent management, and execution. David's game plans help bridge talent gaps that ultimately drive the execution of strategy and competitive innovative national success."

—John Reid, CEO, CATAAlliance (www.cata.ca)

"Leadership is key to the success of just about any organization. The challenge is finding and attracting the 'right' leadership talent. *Hiring Greatness* lays out the steps, in detail and crystal clarity, for meeting this challenge. It is a 'how-to book' par excellence. The authors are true storytellers. They have used their passion and considerable experience to produce a management book that is a real page-turner. There are not many management books that have kept me up reading into the wee hours. *Hiring Greatness* was such a book for me. If you are a business executive and you read one book this year make that book *Hiring Greatness*."

—Ron Wiens, author, *Building Organizations that Leap Tall Buildings in a Single Bound*

"David is a leader in his field with a proven track record applying common sense, achieving success for his clients across a spectrum of disciplines and counties. This book is a culmination of experience, wisdom, perseverance, and results. A must-read."

—Aubrey de Young, Chief Executive Officer, Americas Gateway Development Corporation (Amega Ltda.)

"*Hiring Greatness* is the perfect road map for success in recruiting. So many individuals just fall into the job of recruiting, why not ensure success with deliberate edification? Dive into the latest from Perry and Haluska to uncover what a hiring *professional* really looks like."

—Rayanne Thorn, VP–Marketing for Dovetail Software; editor for intrepidHR; creator and producer, *HR Latte*

"At last! A book on executive search that's easy to read and makes so much sense you feel empowered to take action immediately. *Hiring Greatness* has it all."

—Josef Kadlec, author of the notorious book, *People as Merchandise*

"Making the wrong hiring decision can be detrimental to the organization and those in the hiring process. Money loss is just the tip of the iceberg, the loss of time and emotional intelligence takes a greater toll on everyone. *Hiring Greatness* will allow you to have a clear 'yellow brick road' for success in hiring the right talent for your organization."

—Victor Scapicchio, Adjunct Professor–Organization and Environment, Bentley University

"The essential behind-the-scenes look at the nuts and bolts to recruiting and hiring the next generation of leaders in the twenty-first century. A must-have for Corporate Talent Acquisition leaders, CHROs, and anyone working with ... or around them."

—Gerry Crispin, founder and author, *CareerXroads*

HIRING
GREATNESS

HIRING GREATNESS

HOW TO
Recruit Your Dream Team

AND
Crush the Competition

DAVID E. PERRY
MARK J. HALUSKA

WILEY

Library of Congress Cataloging-in-Publication Data is Available:

Names: Perry, David E., 1960- author. | Haluska, Mark J., 1956- author.
Title: Hiring greatness : how to recruit your dream team and crush the
    competition / David E. Perry, Mark J. Haluska.
Description: Hoboken, New Jersey : John Wiley & Sons, Inc., [2016] | Includes
    bibliographical references and index.
Identifiers: LCCN 2015040820 | ISBN 978-1-119-14-744-2 (cloth);
    ISBN 978-1-119-14-745-9 (ePDF); ISBN 978-1-119-14-746-6 (ePub)
Subjects: LCSH: Employee selection. | Employees–Recruiting. | Personnel
    management. | Success in business.
Classification: LCC HF5549.5.S38 P435 2016 | DDC 658.3/11–dc23 LC record available at
http://lccn.loc.gov/2015040820

Cover Design: Wiley
Cover Image: VICTOR/Getty Images, Inc.
Author (David Perry) photo credit: Eric Laurie

Anita Martel, my partner. With love and admiration.

—D. E. P.

This book is dedicated to all of those potential corporate clients who in my early years in this profession wouldn't give me the time of day; and now that I'm established, to those organizations (today) whose executive search firm preferred vendors' list is comprised of the friends and family plan ...

... you'll never know what Hiring Greatness is!

—M. J. H.

CONTENTS

Contents

How to Maximize Your Use of this Book

We suggest you read it twice. The first time quickly so you appreciate where any information that may be novel to you is. The second time with a highlighter so you can have quick access to information you may be looking to find later.

There are multiple free downloads and extra tools on the site. Make use of what you need. Improve on it and share it with us so we can all work smarter together.

The "Members Only" area holds all the supplemental information. Joining is free and we will never share your information or SPAM you. When prompted for the password, use the password: "Arnold" without the quotation marks.

David and Mark invite you to send your comments and questions here: author@HiringGreatness.com or to our respective company addresses:

David Perry
Managing Partner
www.perrymartel.com
Perry-Martel International Inc.
dperry@perrymartel.com
613.236.6995

Mark Haluska
Founder and Executive Director
www.mjhaluska.com
Realtime Network
haluska@comcast.net
724-495-2733

Hiring Greatness application.

Bonus Online Exclusives to download from www.HiringGreatness .com

□ 'Everything Else You Always Wanted to Know About LinkedIn', by Joe Zinner

□ Executive Search Score Card

□ List of Compensation Items

□ 'Branding for Executive Attraction', by Rayanne Thorn

□ Position Profile for Tulip COO Search

□ Confidential Candidate Brief for Tulip COO Search

□ 'Could Your Tried and True Hiring Practices Expose You to Employment Litigation Guide', by Janette Levey-Frisch, Esq.

FOREWORD

S uccessful recruiting starts with a thorough understanding of the goals, strengths, and needs of the organization.

The most effective executive recruiter is a management consultant to the Search Committee, board, or CEO, an advisor to the company, and a recruiter of talented people who fit the specific needs of the company.

It is not likely to be sufficient to conduct a search with no more known to the executive recruiter than the title of the position to be filled. Success is less likely if the assignment to the executive recruiter is no more than "We need a new CEO," "a COO," "a CFO," or other description of a box on an organization chart. A successful executive recruiter understands that his assignment is to help the company understand its needs, not merely to fill a slot described to the recruiter by the board, CEO, or head of a Search Committee. The most valuable executive recruiter does not simply accept the organization chart presented, but learns the strengths and weaknesses of the people in the organization and advises the company on redesign of the chart to fit the talent found and the goals of the company.

Both the company and executive recruiter must understand the real needs of the organization, the qualities of the right person for the position, the strengths and weaknesses of the officers not being replaced, the quality of the assets of the company, its market position, the short- and long-term goals of the organization, the goals of the board of directors, and need, if any, for a new strategy and vision for success of the organization.

Does the company have a wildly successful strategy but need better execution? Need better financial planning? Need better control of operations? Or does the company need a new vision, new goals, and strategies for achieving those goals? Is the company growing market share or losing share to successful competitors? In each instance, why? Is the company competing in a growing industry with great assets and technology or in a stable or declining industry with little, outdated assets or technology?

Too often executive recruiters have considered little more than the title of the open position, experience in the industry in which the company competes, and prior experience in the same job title.

A great executive recruiter starts his or her work by understanding the needs of the company. While the board or CEO might believe the company needs to replace a departing officer with a person whose prior experience is with the same job title as the officer to be replaced, a great executive recruiter will not accept a search assignment without a better understanding of the needs of the company.

A great executive recruiter is, first, a consultant to or partner with the company in determining the needs of the company and then finding the best person to fit those needs. A great executive recruiter will not accept an assignment unless allowed to first fully participate with the board, CEO, or chair of the Search Committee in deciding the real needs of the company. Success is defined not as "filling an open slot" but as determining the needs of the company, correctly defining the job description, and then filling the position with the best person for the position.

Filling a CEO position presents challenges and opportunities different from other positions. The right CEO can empower his people, create teamwork, and create shareholder value, while a wrong choice of CEO can undermine cooperation between his key people and destroy shareholder value.

The CEO must set strategy and assemble a team of highly qualified people to execute the strategy as a team. Without vision and a well-defined and communicated strategy, the company cannot be expected to flourish. Without a team of talented and qualified people to execute the strategy, the company will be hindered in achieving its goals.

A very smart CEO of a small, young company I was funding years ago told me he could do the job of each of his officers and employees better than each could do their own jobs. Sounded impressive. In a short time I realized it was clear his talents were insufficient to get the job done. The company was growing rapidly but losing substantial amounts of money and did not have acceptable financial controls. I took over as CEO with no prior experience in the industry or as a CEO. My first question was, "What is the role of a CEO?"

The role of a CEO, I decided, was like the role of the conductor of an orchestra. The conductor should not be better at playing any particular instrument than the players could play their instruments. To the contrary, one job of the conductor is to make certain he or she has the very best musicians, each outstanding at playing his or her instrument. The role of the conductor is to assemble the finest musicians, to determine the music to be played, based in part on the capability of the players, and to make certain the players are working together as a team at the pace determined and communicated by the conductor.

The analogy of the conductor of an orchestra well describes the role of a CEO. The CEO must determine strategy (the music to be played), based on the assets of the company (physical assets and the capability of the players), working together as a team at the pace determined and communicated by the CEO.

The company searching for a new CEO and the executive recruiter must understand the role of a CEO to successfully find the best CEO for the company.

It has been my privilege to work with David Perry in searches for executive positions in three companies, one public and two privately held. I have been a member of the board of each of these companies and chair of the Search Committee in one instance. Working with David Perry was a prime example of the role of a great executive recruiter. He started each project with a thorough analysis of the company, its assets, industry position, qualities of its key people, needs for the executive position to be filled, and, based on that analysis, crafted an appropriate job description, plan for execution of the search, and careful screening of potential candidates. The description in this Foreword of a successful executive recruiter is based on my observing David Perry at work and working with him.

Carl Albert, Chairman and Chief Executive Officer,
Fairchild Venture Capital Corporation

PREFACE

There are very few opportunities for a company to improve organizational performance and culture by taking one single, solitary action.

In the six months after Marissa Mayer was hired as Yahoo!'s CEO, the market value of the company increased by $17 billion. Imagine making one decision that created $3.8 million in market value an hour! At nearly the same time Yahoo! began its rapid ascent, Ron Johnson, the new JCPenney CEO, caused sales to plummet—by $4.3 billion. A single decision of his brought losses of $500,000 an hour!

Those are two diametrically opposite examples of how hiring an executive leader can dramatically impact an organization's bottom line. Hire a "star" and you'll win because they'll inspire innovation, invigorate employees, and generate wealth for the company. Choose poorly and you'll suffer serious financial penalties. A bad hire may even mortally wound an organization, with far-reaching consequences. The ripple effect of corporate failure impacts an extensive food chain, from stockholders to customers. These days, no organization survives long without strong leadership.

Organizations today live in a glass pressure cooker with the heat turned on high. An expanding global economy coupled with shareholders who aggressively demand positive financial results at the speed of a Ferrari have driven executive turnover to an all-time high. Not surprisingly, and in exponentially increasing numbers, companies are engaging outside assistance when recruiting senior executives. No one understands more about what it takes to attract key executives than those who make a living talking to them every day.

Professional executive recruiters—or headhunters, as some are known—spend all their time working and negotiating between client organizations and executives. The best executive recruiters understand what it takes to secure the best talent, and what it takes to keep it. Considering the very public results of Yahoo! and JCPenney, it's easy to understand why organizations are increasingly turning to professional executive recruiters to deliver on the critical task of sourcing, vetting, and hiring exceptional executive leadership. The benefits and "simple paybacks" of hiring competent recruiting professionals are significant.

The executive landscape continues to change at an incredible pace. More—and increasingly younger—executives continue to ascend to the C-Suite. They face a fragile and complex global business climate and unforgiving stockholders. Yet they must plot corporate strategy, despite an admitted lack of adequate training for their roles.

In recent years, the global recruitment industry surpassed $590 billion in annual revenues, but that growth often comes at the expense of quality and reliability. Overall, the recruiting profession has a spotty track record when it comes to delivering results. In an industry that regards a 30 percent "stick rate" as successful, the authors truly stand out. "Stick rate" is defined as the rate at which a recently hired executive stays in the position for more than a year, and we've designed a methodology and process that delivers success 99 percent of the time. We're not bragging. It's just a fact.

Like a magician revealing inside secrets to the public, *Hiring Greatness* invites the reader behind the scenes of professional executive recruiting. We'll explain in intimate detail how your organization can learn to discipline itself and adopt a structured and comprehensive approach to its next executive search, and how to avoid the judgment errors that have cost other companies billions of dollars in losses. We will also demonstrate the kind of comprehensive service and expertise you should expect from your Executive Search Professional—should you choose to hire one. To illustrate our approach, we've used the story of David's 1,000th search project as an anecdotal backdrop throughout the book.

David E. Perry and Mark J. Haluska

CHAPTER 1

Great Expectations
Defining Value

Never tell me "the sky's the limit" when there are footprints on the moon.
—Paul Brandt

T he midday flight to L.A. had been uneventful—up, down, no delays. Exactly how I like my flights.

Michael, my designated "second" on this project, drove from the airport. We were both pretty quiet as we limped through the heavy Los Angeles traffic heading toward the client's office in the City of Industry. Going straight there was my idea and Michael was visibly nervous. I guess I should have been too. I had voiced my concerns to Michael on the flight down. I saw no point in stopping at our hotel to rest, let alone unpack, as we might not be there long. Although this was potentially going to be my 1,000th recruiting assignment, Michael knew I wasn't certain we were going to accept the assignment we were heading to discuss. But I'm getting ahead of myself. Let's rewind a week to when our story began.

It was a typical Friday morning. I was halfway through my second cup of coffee. Fridays are always busy: closing out projects, reaffirming next week's meeting itineraries, weekly strategic results review, and so on. For me it's a designated quiet time from 7 to 10 a.m. and the staff knows to hold my calls: no one gets through unless it's an emergency and they know what constitutes an emergency. So when the phone rang I picked it up immediately, expecting to hear my wife or one of my children's voices on the other end.

"Hello," said the stranger's voice. "Is this David Perry, the Rogue Recruiter from the *Wall Street Journal* article?'

"It is!" I replied. "Who am I speaking to and how can I help you this morning?" I replied. Obviously, the "Rogue Recruiter" reference indicated that the caller had read the *Wall Street Journal* article, which revealed some of the more innovative tactics I had employed for successfully contacting elusive and highly desirable senior execs regarding executive search assignments. The *Wall Street Journal* article was a lengthy and revealing piece that had caused quite a stir in the executive search industry. It also brought forth a flood of interest from individuals and companies floundering with their executive recruiting efforts. Even NBC's *Today Show* called requesting an on-air interview.

"Are you the recruiter that did all those crazy things to recruit executives? Was it all true? Are you as good as they say?" he asked.

"Yes," I responded with a laugh. "I am the Rogue Recruiter ... and what can I do for you?"

"My name is Fred Teshinsky. I'm the owner of a manufacturing company, Tulip, in L.A. and I read that article. I need to hire a COO and I've had two companies try—and they both failed: miserable waste of money and my time. So don't you waste my time! Are you really any good?"

Now he had my attention. "Fred, tell me what you do and what the recruiters did for you."

"I told you, I'm a manufacturer. We make products for companies out of plastic. How hard can it be to find a COO in the Midwest with this recession going on anyway?"

Fred and I talked for a good half hour about his company and more specifically why he needed to hire this chief operating officer. At the end of the call I agreed to give him a proposal, and an extensive list of references.

Much to my surprise, Fred phoned all of the references and asked some pretty pointed questions. He was obviously satisfied with the answers because he signed the search agreement and sent the retainer check with two first-class tickets to Los Angeles, as I had requested. I wasn't about to try to resurrect a search that two of the largest firms in the country had failed to deliver on before meeting face-to-face with Fred. That's just asking for trouble. I don't need the headaches and, frankly, in the recruiting business you're only as good as your last hire, and it turns out that my next assignment would be a significant milestone for me.

My business partner Anita Martel had reminded me that the next search I did would be my 1,000th, and I wanted it to go well. Up to that point I had achieved success in 996 out of 999 executive recruiting assignments. So my 1,000th recruiting project was looming, and I didn't want to turn it down until I understood the circumstances that led to failure for the other two firms.

So there we were, crawling through the Los Angeles traffic on our way to meet Fred—and possibly heading straight back home. When we reached our destination we were parked outside a nondescript industrial building made entirely out of cinder block: clean, neat, but certainly nondescript. Apparently, neither the customers nor the owners of the company placed a high priority on the image their building conveyed.

I pushed down hard on the buzzer. It was hot outside and I hoped they had air-conditioning. After a few seconds, somebody, somewhere, must have looked through the video camera to determine that we were okay to let in, and that we were either harmless or lost, because the door was unlocked to allow us to enter. We proceeded into a very small vestibule adorned with wood paneling. The magazines on the coffee tables were all current. I was relieved. The reception area was upscale for a manufacturing facility: That made me feel hopeful that a candidate would not be alienated by an initial bad impression of the office facilities.

No executive recruiter wants to waste his time—or that of a client or prospective candidate—on a wild goose chase. We sell our time and expertise, and it's important to undertake risk mitigation. That's why we were here.

The meeting room we were ushered into up on the second floor was furnished with a massive old mahogany boardroom table. Solid. Heavy. Imposing. With ornately carved high-back black leather chairs. I sensed this boardroom was rarely used for impressing visitors. It was not adorned with pictures of the owners, employees, or the products manufactured. There was nothing personal on the wood-grain paneled walls. I saw the unimpressed look on Michael's face.

For me, though, the modest digs were a good sign. I prefer to deal with companies that focus on producing quality for their customers and aren't unnecessarily obsessed with image. Personally I gravitate to companies that solve real world problems, not ones that spend a lot of time and money on fluff. The boardroom was functional and had seen lots of traffic over the years. It felt solid. This company was real.

Fred came in. He's a short guy, and was favoring his left leg. He was followed by three other gentlemen who turned out to be retired executives sitting on Fred's board of directors. Fred introduced himself first, then turned toward the three gentlemen and introduced each of them quickly by name only. I would learn their pedigrees later over lunch. Fred was gregarious and welcoming, inquiring about our flight and how we found the directions getting here.

I introduced myself and Michael and then turned to Fred and said, "Let's begin. I need to ask you three questions."

Perhaps he was startled by my forwardness, but Fred fired back, "You work for me now, and I'll be asking the questions."

What followed sent a waterfall of perspiration gushing forth from Michael's balding head.

"Oh really!" I said. Reaching into the inside pocket of my suit jacket I held out the envelope Fred used to send our signed agreement and check. I quickly produced a single slip of paper and held it up for Fred's inspection, saying, "This is your check, which I haven't cashed. I'm going to ask you the three questions. If you answer them correctly we will take the search. If you don't, we won't, and I'll rip through the signature box, return the check, and we can all go for an early lunch. Fair enough?" I didn't bother to wait for his response.

"First question. Fred, I understand you hired not one but two of the top search firms in America to find your chief operating officer and they both came up empty. Did they give you a hands-off list before starting?"

"A what? What's that?" was Fred's response.

"Fred, did the search consultant present any of your competitors' people, or were most of the people you interviewed consultants?" I quickly asked as question number two.

Fred shook his head and was about to speak when I interrupted him and asked, "Fred, did either search firm provide a written plan detailing their approach to filling the search? Did they provide a Talent Road Map?"

"No," was all Fred said.

Now, by this time Michael's breathing sounded a little labored. Indeed, Michael was new to the search business. This was the first time I had taken him with me to visit a potential new client, as we had only recently started working together. Michael had been my client.

He had been a very successful high-tech executive for more than 40 years—a professional engineer and master negotiator. Michael had risen through the ranks to become chief executive officer of several large companies and two start-ups. Michael is a brilliant engineer and solid chief executive officer. Under his leadership his last company had literally gone from worst to first (dead last in their space) and into an acquisition in less than a year.

When Michael started twisting my arm to let him join Perry-Martel and become an Executive Search Professional (ESP), I was only too pleased at the prospect. Michael had the experience of several hundred hires under his belt by this time and certainly had the moxie! We had gotten off to a fast start working on two critical hires together and he was soaking it all in. But looking at him right then and there, I knew he didn't approve of my reaction to Fred. Clearly he was thinking, "You're nuts. We just flew 3,000 miles for a meeting that lasted less than six seconds and now you're going to rip up his check and go home?" It was a priceless moment—for me, at least.

"We'll take the search and complete it," I said as I pivoted around to face Fred. "Fred, I'm pretty certain that most of your competitors' best executives didn't even know you had a search going. Further, in terms of attracting top-level executive talent, I don't think the fault lies with your company. I'll tell you exactly why the first two search firms were unsuccessful and why neither firm should have taken your money: because that's all they did … take your money. The previous executive searches haven't worked out because you were only getting access to a limited segment of the entire executive talent pool. The options those firms were presenting to you were likely significantly limited by the hands-off restrictions they were ethically bound by. And you just confirmed they didn't disclose any limitations that might compromise the search. That's one drawback to working with the larger search firms. Since they deal with thousands of different companies every year, they're often restricted from approaching any executives from companies the search firms have done business with during the previous 12 to 24 months. It's very likely that, because the two firms you hired where among the largest in the USA, many of the firms you would have liked to talk to people from were on that list. Both firms should have informed you about which of your competitors they could not approach."

I felt confident the search hadn't really been done thoroughly because I understand the restrictions ethical search firms are under with regards to "poaching" from their clients. While the ethics are commendable, in this case it drastically reduced the resource pool the search consultants could draw from—yet they didn't disclose this to Fred. It's professionally sloppy, at best, that neither search firm disclosed the limitations of their search options. They should have. I respect such agreements as well, but because I'm a boutique firm and highly selective in choosing clients, I have significantly fewer hands-off restrictions on my searches. I also spend considerably more time vetting both the client and the candidate to ensure a realistic and well-defined mandate targeted at a scrupulously vetted list of candidates.

In any case, we spent the next two hours speaking with Fred and his board of directors to get a clear idea of exactly what was needed in the role now and after Fred retired. This was simultaneously a succession planning exercise for the CEO role. We focused on competitive issues around the business; where the plastics manufacturing industry was; what impacted their competitiveness; how its customers bought; and what the board felt the company needed to maintain their lead. But what I really wanted to figure out was: which executive out there was made for this company? Who was Fred's professional soulmate, the "one" who shared his vision and sensibility as if he or she was destined by fate to sit at that mahogany table and not miss a beat.

Because every executive search project is very much like arranging a marriage—an economic marriage. It requires mutual respect, transparency, maturity, and the near-certainty of a good fit on both sides. The goal isn't simply to fill the position. It can't be. Otherwise I'll end up having to do the same search six months later, and that's not something I particularly enjoy (or have to do very often, considering our 99.97 percent success rate). That's why we can guarantee the executives for 12 months following a placement. It's also why I value my candidates and their needs just as much, if not more, than the companies who pay me to find them. The process has to be "bottom up" and, ultimately, about making a good match: otherwise it's much more likely to end in failure, which can result in wasted money for the company and a stalled or even ruined career for the candidate.

Indeed, the technical aspects of executive searches are usually fairly straightforward. The key to success lies in the subtleties of the pairing. We've recruited executives at every size of company: early-stage companies, small- and medium-sized businesses, billion-dollar multinationals and Fortune 500 companies. And no matter what stage of growth, no matter the market, you need to appraise the company's culture—and determine the best fit for both the firm and the executive—to ensure you understand what works, what doesn't, and why in all cases.

WHY HIRING GREATNESS MATTERS

Picking a person is the most important business decision you'll make. What's an employee worth? Not compensation-wise—but *value-wise*.

As an extreme example, entertainer David Bowie floated a personal bond issue a few years ago. He offered investors a portion of his future royalties from previously recorded material and receipts from future concerts. The "Bowie Bonds" were gone within an hour of the offer, for more than $50 million.

In an even more striking case, when Dreamworks SKG went public investors immediately drove the value of its bonds to $2 billion. Dreamworks was a film studio without a studio, a film, or even a star. All it had was the intangible value of its founders: Steven Spielberg, Jeffrey Katzenberg, and David Geffen.

The *intangible value of being*—that's what the new knowledge economy is all about. Veteran information age guru Stan Davis has confirmed the increasing value of people in today's economy.

A person's value is just a measure of how much someone is willing to pay to obtain something from them.

In their book *Blur*, Davis and Meyer point out that the boundaries between your work and home life are disappearing.[1] In fact, today the rate of change and the depth of connectivity are so fast that every person, product, service, and company are blurring together. Computerization and communications have made us all a linked community. There are, for example, nine times more computer processors in our products than in our computers—9 billion CPUs in items like phones, hotel keys, consumer electronics, day planners, and cars.

As products become more software-driven, they also become easier to link together. Intelligence and information have become the key value being offered in a consumable (some 90 percent of the value of a new car is estimated to be in the computers and software). And you are the value-adder.

Instead of resources or land, "capital" today means human capital. It doesn't take a shoe factory to go into the shoe business these days. Nor do you need raw materials or fleets of trucks. Nike became a shoe industry leader by concentrating on the value-producing capacity of its employees for design, marketing, and distribution know-how. The real capital is intangible: the person's knowledge level, combined with an aptitude for application and execution.

Today, employees—in the high-technology world especially—tend to think of themselves as "free agents." Like a professional athlete who is always in training, knowledge workers are continuously investing in the next set of skills and training, driving up their personal "stock price." This puts knowledge value in the driver's seat.

Employers, like yourself, will try ever harder to retain smart, boldly entrepreneurial overachievers.

Google used stock options to attract exactly this kind of person, and has created thousands of employee millionaires. Apple employees who contributed the maximum to Apple's employee stock purchase plan (ESPP) have seen their shares grow in value to approximately $1,112,189 over the seven years—that's 635.76 percent.[2]

In this world, *value* is not *salary*—not for the employer and not for the employee. Your search for a star candidate should be value-focused, not salary-driven.

The authors, both experienced Executive Search Professionals, understand how to look for *knowledge value*. And just as you'd expect from the complexity of the human factors involved, it is an intensive process. What we bring to the table is a set of guidelines developed from years of experience in locating just such value, and the experience that lets us apply these guidelines quickly on your behalf.

We know what's important for today's knowledge workers—be they executives or programmers—and we bring these elements together and explain them for you in this book.

In the "olden days" (10 years ago) a leadership search was like a two-dimensional board game. It allowed a company a leisured amount of time to send out requests for résumés, which could then be judged along a price/performance set of axes. It allowed for a precise, two-dimensional grid, and a search process so structured and simple that judgments could be handled by a corporate HR department's less-skilled skilled staff.

Now the world moves in three dimensions, at a speed more resembling a video game. It's zap or get zapped, in real time. In such a fast-paced dogfight, you need to define your missions very carefully: no wasted energy, no blurred vision. The right people are even more important to find than ever before.

You need a team of people who think in three dimensions. Nothing else will do.

You need a seasoned recruiter who will be your success partner, who can think in terms of a fast-action, complex world.

Our methodology is based on a "value grid." The grid identifies the value that a candidate can bring to your company, and then matches the candidate's value systems to your own requirements to ensure a perfect fit.

We apply three measures, or axes, to deliver a successful skill set to your company. There are three dimensions of human value that work as a framework, whether you're hiring or being hired.

The three dimensions to recruit talent, by assessing the *value of an individual's* contribution, are shown in Figure 1.1.

Hiring Greatness

Height of Value	Know what's important. What value contribution does your company need? How do you evaluate the worth of someone's contribution?
Sight of Value	Find what's important. Where can you find the precise combination of skills and values and proactively identify the ideal candidates?
Flight of Value	Get what's important. How can you attract that talent to land in your company?

Figure 1.1 Three dimensions of value.

HEIGHT OF VALUE: KNOWING WHAT'S IMPORTANT

The production of value is the most important criterion of hiring and should be your most important. Value is not salary and worth doesn't flow from a job title. Knowing what's important to a company means looking beyond job titles and compensation tables, especially in the knowledge-based economy where sudden changes and uncertainty are the norm.

Knowing how to evaluate the worth of someone's contribution is the important element. Being able to assess a candidate's star performance capabilities is the key between average and extraordinary. There are two elements you need to consider:

1. Understanding thoroughly what the value contribution is that you want, and;

2. Understanding how you'll know when you find it.

Today's executives are on the edge of change, and they see better than anyone else how their worth measures up.

What is the *value* you're looking for from an employee's contribution to your company?

Especially for its senior positions, a company is rarely looking to fill in a tick-box on a standard employee recruitment form. Usually, companies are looking for something more nebulous and important. You're looking for a senior person who can deliver a *quality*, not a quantity. Instead of filling in a box, you're looking to explode out from an open-ended, initiative-driven space.

Qualities are difficult to find, measure, or test in an ordinary recruitment drive. And you don't find those qualities by searching for specific salary levels—the qualities that make up the *New Value Table* are money-resistant.

The New Value Table

The qualities that create value for your company are shown in Figure 1.2.

YOUR CORE VALUE REQUIREMENTS	QUALITIES THAT DELIVER THE VALUE
1. Create new intellectual wealth for my company; add to my intellectual assets.	1. A relentless desire to make something new; to cut a new path rather than take a road.
2. High-energy enthusiasm for the job, regardless of the hours worked.	2. Work is a game—an integral, vibrant part of his or her life.
3. The money is not only not the most important issue — it's beside the point.	3. Internal pride to leave a "legacy signature" on their work, rather than strive for a paycheck.
4. Enduring performance.	4. An ability to stay and finish the race, because not finishing is inconceivable emotionally.
5. "Think around corners" to creatively problem-solve.	5. Has an inner voice saying, "There's always a way [to create a technology fix: make a deal]"
6. Brings up-to-date professionalism into every fray.	6. Contains a desire to grow professionally—to become the best person he or she can be: invests in him- or herself.
7. Ever-increasing contribution.	7. The key to inner pleasure is recognized as making an individual contribution.
8. Identifies and develops values for your company.	8. Instinctive grasp and exploitation of today's real value: the intangible capital of brand image, staff talent, and customer relationships.

Figure 1.2 The new value table.

You need to match the value you require to the qualities of special candidates. Knowing the nuts and bolts of the industry is not enough. It requires taking the time to get to know the inner workings of your company: its products, people, and culture.

This goes beyond skill sets and résumés. You want professionals whose *qualities* match your value requirements. You should share a similar vision. Only then will there be a successful fit for you, your candidate, and your future growth prospects.

SIGHT OF VALUE: FINDING WHAT'S IMPORTANT

More than ever in our history, huge value is being leveraged from smart ideas—and the winning technology and business models they create. So the people who can deliver them are becoming invaluable, and methods of employing and managing them are being transformed.

The candidates you're looking for aren't looking for you. They already have jobs, almost certainly a good job. They aren't scanning the "Careers" section.

So how do you find someone who doesn't raise a hand and say, "Here I am"?

The Location Process: The Old Way

As my friend Joe Zinner, from Zinner and Company Leadership Search, always says, "There are two kinds of candidates in the job market: People who are running *from* something and people who are running *to* something! Advertising and job boards typically yield the unemployed, the unhappy, and most often the unqualified applicants."

Lame and Tame Approaches

Everyone has heard the recruiting call that starts "…who do you know…." This is the hallmark of an inexperienced recruiter, hoping you'll say, "Why that person you described is me and I'd love to meet your client…."

This overused ploy today nets the response, "I don't know anyone ... " and a prompt hang-up. Such a conventional and unimaginative approach ends quickly and doesn't garner the recruiter any opportunity to present the career pitch, pique their interest, or qualify their background. Prospective candidates hang up quickly because the recruiter is deemed to be "light." This doesn't afford the recruiter the option to repackage and represent the offer.

There Is an Alternative ...

Candidates are more sophisticated than ever and expect recruiters to be professional and knowledgeable. So many people now manage their own careers aggressively, and if they're going to talk to a recruiter they want someone who can talk to them, their industry, and their challenges.

As a recruiter you need instant credibility, spontaneous bonding, and respect in less than 30 seconds—on your first phone call.

You need staying power and the ability to repackage and re-present an opportunity around a candidate's needs.

Recruiters can't afford to waste a prospect with the hackneyed "who do you know" question. Because they do know! Winners know they're winners, but aren't going to waste time telling you that. So a potential candidate for your organization will get turned off in disdain by an old approach.

Traditional recruiters are actually human relations amateurs, and that's why the placement industry has such a high turnover. These unprepared people get shot down in flames by yet another prospect before they even get a chance to tell the story of the opportunity.

Today, Science!

Research must underpin a search project. The upfront work is often laborious, even tedious, and not enjoyed by many search professionals who simply want to sell the project.

But good research makes you able to tightly target your prospects. Hone the message and deliver it to the right individual. Then you're able to speak from a reference point of knowledge about them, their company, their industry, their challenges, and therefore emphasize the positives of your opportunity.

You bond instantly. You develop a relationship. You're trusted. You're an advisor they refer to their friends and associates even when unasked.

The process has changed to one of scarcity. Now all candidates are scarce and demographics will keep it this way. The good ones are being hidden by their company's management and are incented to stay. They need to be wooed.

They need to be enticed in the most professional manner possible.

How?

First you have to select a career opportunity that's interesting. Not an easy feat. You need to ask the clients the hard questions beyond, "Why should someone take this job?" to really understand the business drivers: their market pressures; their culture inside and outside the boardroom; the dynamic beyond a snapshot in time of your current needs.

You need to understand the career implications and be able to relate them to a complete stranger—often thousands of miles away—who is happy, productive, and achieving for someone else.

It takes more than four minutes on the phone to do that.

This is a proprietary process that sets up the "close" from beginning to end. And that process is painstakingly thorough—because it's your future we're creating.

FLIGHT OF VALUE: GET WHAT'S IMPORTANT

It's Not Always about the Money

How you attract and land the star candidate you want requires more than a checkbook. Without overpaying for the identified value, how do you meet the needs of the human being you're dealing with? What value requirements does he or she have that you could fill?

- For many top performers it's not about money … Facebook, LinkedIn, Tesla, SpaceX … it's about changing the world.

- Cofounders Larry Page and Sergey Brin brought Google to life in September 1998 as a means to find information faster on the web.

- Steve Jobs is the entrepreneurial creation myth writ large: he cofounded Apple in his parents' garage in 1976, was ousted in 1985, returned to rescue it from near-bankruptcy in 1997, and by the time he died, in October 2011, had built it into the world's most valuable company. Along the way he helped transform seven industries: personal computing, animated movies, music, phones, tablet computing, retail stores, and digital publishing.[3]

Today's knowledge workers don't want to be managed. They want to lead and be trusted. They need to be empowered with the right information to make sound decisions, to grow the business and to be part of a community that is contributing to something worthy of their time and energy.

Listen and Learn Now

In literally thousands of pages of articles, research documents, and interview transcripts, what comes through loud and clear is that the knowledge industry, in its battle for human resources, has stagnated into a bidding war where the only winner is the company with the deepest pockets.

"Shrimp wars," signing bonuses, golden handcuffs, gift baskets, three raises a year, beer fridges, pool tables, planes towing banners, booths set up at gardening shows, paid tuition, options, flexi-hours, the list goes on—when does it all stop and at what point does one realize that the war, fought in this way, is lost already?

Those companies with the highest profile—Apple, General Electric, Google, et al.—have already won. And they'll continue to win until a company like yours either changes the rules, or plays the game differently.

It's Not the Money

The people you're after, be they chief executive officers or product managers, define who they are by what they do and where they do what they do. There's nothing they love more than facing a challenge and accomplishing what's never been accomplished before. It's how they work, play, and compete among themselves.

Being a company structured in such a way that allows the individual to succeed, as part of a team of top performers, is the key to attracting people.

Is This Person Familiar?

Let's look at some of the characteristics of our target audience, by tracking a typical candidate:

In high school, "jocks" defined who they were by their athletic prowess, the "beautiful people" by their looks and charisma, and "geeks" by their seeming solitude, introverted nature, and tape-repaired glasses. The geeks weren't the fastest or strongest and certainly weren't the most popular, but they were the smartest. They took pride in knowing that while the athlete was up collecting his trophy, they were the ones tutoring him in math.

When our geek—let's call him Corey—moved from high school to university, he found an environment in business, computer science, or engineering, which embraced who he is. He was also, for the first time in his life, surrounded by hundreds of like-minded souls. Nirvana.

But Corey soon realized that this new environment came with a down side: The bar was raised. He wasn't necessarily the "smartest kid in the class" anymore. Now he had competition.

Oddly enough, Corey thrived in this environment because, in a way he really is no different from an athlete. He's driven to improve his times, his scores; he's driven to get around barriers; he's driven to go places no one has gone before. University, and the work environment he was about to enter, wants people who are competitive and Corey always pushed to find if he had what it took.

Over the course of time Corey evolved from the introverted, computer-obsessed person he was to a still somewhat quiet, confident person who realizes the interests he's had for so long are now highly sought after. He's realized he can share his dreams, and his journey, with a company that wants people just like him.

Location, Location, Location

"Coreys" define themselves not only by what they do, but also where they do what they do.

People like Corey know the money will come. They know they're highly sought after, and that should they choose to leave a company in the morning, often, that same morning, they'll be hired by someone else. This is challenging because the leverage of money that most companies use to attract people doesn't work with this group. They're looking for more.

The person we want to speak to wants to be the best, be perceived as the best, and wants to change the world. A lot of this will be defined not only by what he or she does, but where he or she does what he or she does. There are companies out there with so much cachet that employees want people to know where they work. They're proud of working for the company and want to identify themselves with it.

The "I"s Have It

Although our audience wants to "buy in," they also are very individualistic. We believe it's largely because of where they've come from. High performance people want to be part of an elite team, but also want to make an individual difference. The power of individual accomplishment within an organization is one of the single most important strategic elements that must come through in a pitch. People—the people we want to talk to—need to know, for selfish and unselfish reasons, that they can make a difference.

One of the most startling things in our industry was an employee survey that indicated people don't actually want to move around: As long as they can believe they're working for and with the best, they're happy to stay. Likewise, one of the key elements employees look for is the training offered at a company. Essentially, what training seems to mean to these people is "marketability," should they need or want to leave a company. What both these issues say to us is people need and want stability. People would rather deal with change in the job they do, not where they do that job.

Shrimp Wars - The Price of Playing

By and large the whole industry plays by the same rules and, occasionally, someone does something interesting. It seems the following incentives are the price of admission for companies looking for new hires:

- Signing bonuses

- Multiple annual raises

- Options and restricted stock

- A great work environment

- A courtship process that would woo the most coy lover

But ...

Every company that promotes itself effectively must make both a logical and emotional connection with the consumer. The needs of the recruit must be reflected at both an emotional and logical level. The company shouldn't present itself as boring, staid, or traditional, but as an emotionally based image of dynamism, youth, and forward movement. The emotional appeal of a company offering individual meaning, status, and project glory can upset the conventional offers of conventional players. We need look no further than the New Economy companies who have grown successful in a short period of time.

Our audience is smart, educated, motivated, and in possession of an inordinate amount of business savvy that their predecessors lacked. They represent the elite of the work force. Every company in every country wants them.

So recruiting executive talent today requires:

- The ability to microtarget the competition's employees where they live, not where they work

- The occasion to treat each potential candidate as an individual, providing a customized response tailored to their needs

- A value proposition—*like an elevator pitch*—focused on their needs

That's how you Hire Greatness and increase your value.

THE "PERFECT STORM"

I encourage companies to use Executive Search Professionals under the right conditions, which I will now explain.

Let's look at a typical scenario where the decision to outsource recruiting and use an Executive Search Professional (ESP) is imminently critical.

You're a member of the senior management team of a successful business. You are profitable, but top line growth isn't what you or your board would like to see. You have both entrenched and emerging competitors. You meet with your fellow management team members and decide you must expand your product management, product development, sales, and ultimately support personnel. You collectively develop a budget for the acquisition and employment of these resources, and at the suggestion of your human resource (HR) organization, assume minimal outside recruiting help (if any at all) with the exception of a few contingency recruiters.

Your HR organization feels confident they can staff these positions on a timely basis and demonstrate their strategic value to the team. The senior team then presents the plan to the board, who want to see a return on investment and understand how the company's size, market reach, and valuation should be impacted. They not only approve your proposal, but encourage you to move quickly because they have extreme concerns about the new and emerging competitors entering the marketplace. The stage is set for the recruiting "perfect storm." (Personal note: Every executive hire should be judged on its return on investment—ROI is not just for capital expenditures.)

Your HR manager meets with the hiring authorities and develops a brief description of the individuals required. He or she then looks at existing job descriptions and determines titles and compensation from the long-standing company compensation plan. Having identified the individuals, he or she checks back with the hiring authorities who really "don't have time" to review and will assume they can sort it out when they interview candidates.

The HR organization then moves forward as planned: advertising, posting to various job boards, and encouraging employees to submit suggestions from their networks. Because the market is growing, they are inundated with résumés. These are mostly from people who aspire to become the individual you're looking for, but are far earlier in their career and lack experience. There are also key skills dealing either with specific functional responsibilities or new markets not emphasized in the generic write-ups that were posted on the job boards. Remember: The best executives aren't looking on job boards. The result is a flood of ambitious underqualified and overqualified individuals and, for the few who are qualified, an inability to attract them given the compensation that has been (based on history and not current market conditions) set from the opening.

This goes on for about three months, which brings you to your next board meeting. The board is still anxious about competition and wants to know how you're progressing with your expansion. The truthful answer is: You *aren't*, and you *won't* until you change the way you're approaching it. This fact leads to some difficult discussions and frustration on the part of the CEO and senior management team, and raises concerns with the board.

Now you look at the more senior positions and say, "Perhaps we should look outside for additional recruiting talent to support our overloaded HR organization" (who are sorting through thousands and thousands of résumés, all of low value, trying to save cost). This brings us to what kind of recruiters to choose, and what selection criteria you'll use to pick one. For the more senior positions, you and the team choose to look for an ESP who will help you fill the most critical openings quickly.

As in every profession, ESPs fit on a performance continuum from low to high. Your collective task is to find one on the high end of the scale. Bear in mind that unless you and the other senior managers involved interview the prospective recruiters, and also assume the role of ultimate decision maker in selecting an ESP, this task will likely be handed off to your HR or purchasing department. More often than not, they'll be habitually inclined to find the lowest price alternative. Alternately, they may run to the largest firms, where they'll pay full fee for a severely limited candidate pool. And, in the case of HR, finding the "right search firm" assures they regain whatever "political juice" they may have lost by not making any progress to date. The selection of an ESP must have senior management involvement.

Unfortunately, using a competitive bid strategy to select an ESP may compromise the value proposition of the search. The collaborative level of corporate commitment required in the successful executive "recruitment and hiring cycle" requires significant time, energy, patience, and cooperation. It requires the priority dedication of human and financial resources to a level that matches the urgency of the task. This might not be the time or place to bargain hunt—drilling down deeper than price should be your first order of business when comparing ESPs. If executed correctly, the ESP investment will achieve simple payback with meteoric speed. Your recruiter should establish his or her value, disclose his or her limitations, and delineate the comprehensive process he or she will follow in your search. He or she must consistently demonstrate his or her expertise and drive the process to a successful conclusion.

So, whereas return on investment (ROI) is always important, beware the low fee or "recruiting mill" arrangement. Low cost may equate to low value. It is apropos to say that "*true ESPs have to personally, and by hand, shovel tons of coal to find the perfect diamond.*" Recruiting mills dig fast, but not deep. Their employees make a living by handling large volumes of concurrent searches, often by simply throwing résumés at their clients as fast as they can until something sticks. Beware, lest they get the gold and you get the shaft.

Similarly, beware the automatic assumption that it's always best to use the largest search firms with domain dominance. If they have domain experience, they also likely have many companies in the space they're barred from recruiting from. As in Fred's case, defaulting to the largest firms might actually limit your choices by eliminating ideal candidates and may also force the search farther afield, usually raising the compensation cost, introducing relocation cost, and lengthening the recruiting process.

Recapping the scenario we've constructed, your principal issues are timing; adequacy of the job description; adequacy of the compensation; and involvement of the management team in the process. A true ESP will identify these issues very quickly and help you sort through it. Most retained ESPs have held senior-level positions in a variety of companies and have often had P&L responsibility. If you lowball the fees, credible ESPs will outline where the value resides in their fee structure. They will guarantee the executive for at least 12 months so they have a vested interest in ensuring that the right hire is made. There is far more to a successful recruiting agreement than just the fee. This is not the place for average.

Amid all this stress, you and the other team members desperately need a method to objectively evaluate your alternatives and quickly move forward before your competitors sense your hesitation. For your convenience we have provided a set of key questions and considerations to help you select an ESP and his or her firm after you've inquired about the firm's hands-off companies. (And I do mean the firm's hands-off companies and *not* just the individual consultant's—ethically they should be the same, because if that firm will raid from their other clients, they'll also recruit people away from your company.) It should also help you understand the value they bring and where it's required. The ESP you select will represent your company when they talk to candidates, competitors, suppliers, and other players in the marketplace, along with profiling your company in enticing the candidate to interview for the job. Remember most people on job boards are either unemployed or constantly seeking employment. The ESP will help you find those who are already employed and who are more than capable of meeting your organization's requirements, and in the aggregate at a far lower actual or opportunity cost.

If you're now actively considering retaining an ESP we urge you to read the following four questions. If the search firm passes muster, download the free Executive Search Score Card available on the website at www.HiringGreatness.com. Asking the additional 21 questions will help ensure your search is handled by professionals and is executed in a timely manner.

Executive search score card.

The Four Critical Questions to Ask an Executive Search Professional (ESP) Before Hiring

1. Is the ESP free from restrictions in terms of recruiting executives from your direct competitors if necessary?

You need to know if the search firm's hands-off list unreasonably restricts your pool of potential companies. Determine if the list excludes some or all of the firms you would want to look at for executive leadership. If they do, you must determine if they're still able to meet your needs. Some of the big firms are so large they can't ethically recruit from tens of thousands of organizations, so if your best candidates would ideally come from a competitor, you would be wise to ensure the ESP doesn't have a hands-off agreement with any of them. Otherwise, they won't be able to ethically touch their employees. Ethics matter greatly to search professionals. None will risk an ongoing relationship with an established client to feed a new account. Our best advice: Ask for a list and check it.

I don't understand why anyone would steal from a client, but the practice was commonplace when I started recruiting 30 years ago. Since then, the industry has come a long way in cleaning up its public image. But the downside of that is when you choose one of the large search firms you may be limiting your reach into companies you want to go into. The math is simple: A company serving 1,000 clients per year has 1,000 fewer companies they can go to present your opportunity. Clients of the search firm have the expectation, often with legal recourse, of not having their staff approached by the recruiting firm for opportunities elsewhere, often for two years. This narrows your candidate pool by 2,000 companies every year on a rolling forward basis, and is one of

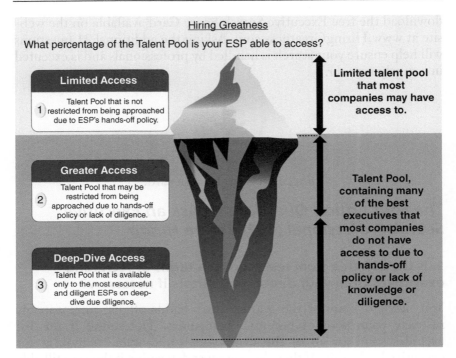

Figure 1.3   Executive talent pool.

the worst things about hiring a firm that specializes in a particular vertical: the smaller the market, the more restrictive the hands-off rules. Now imagine how shallow the talent pool (Figure 1.3) becomes with a firm servicing 10,000 companies a year. Bigger does not necessarily mean better—it may mean the exact opposite. Ask for a list of hands-off companies before you engage a consultant, and determine for yourself if the firm will be too restricted.

The two firms Fred had previously engaged represented roughly 40,000 companies on their respective hands-off lists. It was clear from my tone that I felt the firms should have told Fred about this, and that neither firm should have taken the search given the limited pool of potential candidates available. When dealing with search firms, you need to quantify the risk by obtaining disclosure on competitive restrictions.

2. Does the ESP understand the role you need to fill?

A good executive search firm will help you refine the position description based on their market knowledge. Starting with a clear candidate road map—which all parties have agreed to after participating in its creation—is critical to your success. Investing in the front-end definitions of role, responsibilities, and demonstration of achievements will produce superior results.

TIP

It's impossible to understand an organization's culture from a job description, and trial and error recruiting takes too much time. Your ESP can only gauge a candidate's fit if they've invested time with several members of your organization and performed a benchmarking interview. Also, quickly conducting a candidate benchmarking exercise (more on this in Chapter 4) will go a long way to ensuring you and your consultant understand what's required from a skills and chemistry/cultural fit.

3. Will an experienced ESP actually perform the search?

Typically, a firm's representative will be their most polished business development person (a knife and fork salesperson) who may have a decade's worth of experience but play no ongoing role in the search. There are many firms that will put a team onto your assignment and, while this may sound great, this team may be comprised of very junior people learning the ropes. Often they're freshly minted MBA grads.

I can't overemphasize that it is critical to ascertain precisely *who* will perform the search. Before you sign any agreement, you must meet the person responsible for delivering your project successfully—and if it's a team, you'll want to meet all the players. Ensure you're comfortable with the specific recruiter assigned to the project if they're not the same as the person who sold you the project. Key to your success is the individual who first makes contact with a prospective recruit. It's not uncommon for a senior executive to decline when called for the first time. After all, he or she is busy and successful, likely has a great job, and isn't actively looking for work.

Your success depends on understanding what happens with that potential candidate next. Early in my career I made a very good living as the "recruiter of last resort," brought in to rescue stalled or failed searches. Most times I recruited an executive who had already been dropped from consideration weeks or months earlier simply because he or she declined the first approach. If at first they say "No," should the prospect be dropped—or should another attempt be made? If so, how? When? Why? Your ESP must have the savvy to skillfully reignite the interest of a candidate who has already dismissed the opportunity. When considering an ESP, ask for specific examples of how they may have resurrected such candidates in the past.

> In one instance, it personally took me 51 phone calls—each time leaving a unique voicemail message—to entice a divisional president from Motorola into considering an opportunity. I was working with a smallish start-up, which absolutely needed his specific set of skills and Rolodex. There were always other candidates, but none were as ideally qualified. Regrettably he was very busy and quite happy where he was. Fortunately, we had enough runway and, following an extended six-month "courtship," he accepted the role and led a very successful IPO.

4. Does the firm offer a performance guarantee?

Every time you do a search you need to protect your investment against two possible scenarios: (1) no suitable candidate is found, or (2) the selected candidate doesn't work out. Either scenario could leave you with an unfilled position despite having paid a full fee. Ask about guarantees up front.

Scenario #1: The search firm presents several slates of candidates, *all* of whom you deem to be unacceptable. Will the firm continue searching until they find a suitable candidate or will they walk away? You need to ensure they're in it for the long haul. By the way, this is another excellent reason to benchmark a candidate soon after the project gets started so you don't waste time and lose momentum or the element of surprise with your competitors.

TIP

You can tell a lot about the firm by the amount of up-front due diligence they do defining the requirement—the more, the better.

Scenario #2: The selected candidate doesn't work. What's the warranty period? There's no industry consensus on that, so it's typically a negotiated term. You should be certain to put it in the signed agreement. A guarantee could be as short as 30 (calendar) days or as long as six months. You probably already know how long it takes your people to judge a new executive's competency, so make sure you either get the search firm to cover your investment for that amount of time or shorten your assessment program so you're covered in case of a bad hire. Determine up front what an appropriate period of time is for your company—one year is not unreasonable. Also, discuss what extra charges, if any, you may incur. It's also not unreasonable for direct costs associated with the search to be billed if the firm needs to redo the search from scratch.

The time to discuss these issues is before the beginning of the ESP relationship and, most certainly, before you commence a search. Finding great leadership at the CEO or executive level is complex. It requires a firm with a breadth of experience in completing senior executive assignments. It requires critical thinking and problem solving skills, and a proactive and fresh approach to each assignment because even the most successful searches are filled with challenges. The active involvement of the Search Committee Chair throughout the process is pivotal to insuring a high-quality result.

There are yet more questions you need to ask, which we'll cover in further chapters. But first, we suggest you download the Executive Search Score Card referenced earlier in this chapter from the book's website, www.HiringGreatness.com.

NOTES

1. Stan Davis and Christopher Meyer, *Blur: The Speed of Change in the Connected Economy* (New York: Warner Books, 1998).
2. www.forbes.com/sites/troyonink/2011/10/19/1-1-million-for-apple-employees/.
3. https://hbr.org/2012/04/the-real-leadership-lessons-of-Steve-jobs.

CHAPTER 2

Architects of Success
Setting Up the Search Committee

One of the tests of leadership is the ability to recognize a problem before it becomes an emergency.

—Arnold Glasow

Next, all of us assembled for a tour of the facility. Fred stopped frequently to greet employees along the way. It was clear from the top floor to the shop floor Fred was the patriarch of Tulip. Well respected and admired, his would be big shoes to fill. As we observed them interact it became obvious the staff were almost like family. Many people had been with the company for decades.

That type of loyalty and respect can't be bought or faked. Fred knew his employees' families well, and frequently referenced children and events that were important to his employees' lives as we toured the office and manufacturing floor. Whomever we hired needed to understand this intimate relationship Fred had with his people, along with realizing they couldn't replace Fred. Rather, they needed to appreciate how to nurture these relationships for the benefit of the business.

Before heading to lunch with Fred and the board, we explained what else we needed to know, why we needed to know it, and how we were going to proceed. At lunch Michael and I focused on two objectives: assessing how Fred and his board members worked together, and choosing a Search Chair.

Michael focused on assessing relationships among the board members themselves, since they would comprise our Search Committee. It was his job to gauge how they interacted. Was there a

29

dominant board member? Did they have a healthy respect for Fred? How did they discuss ideas among themselves? Talking about politics normally brings out any differences and shows any rigidity in thinking.

I was most interested in identifying a Search Chair because I was *not* going to report to Fred for the duration of the search. I know my character all too well, and thought our personal working styles would clash. I've met many Freds over the years: brilliant, high functioning engineering types who want to know every single detail—every day—so they can help. Of course, I couldn't blame him for wanting to keep a close eye on me and his money. He wanted to be successful the third time round, and help out wherever possible ... at least until he was comfortable we knew what we were doing. I would have done the same thing in his shoes, but I don't work well that way. I certainly didn't have the time to call with daily updates, nor did he have time to deal with them. As I would explain to them later, you don't want to have the CEO (or whomever becomes the ultimate hiring authority) distracted from running the business. In these cases, a Search Chair is clearly the best way to go.

At lunch, it quickly became apparent that board member Carl Albert would make the best Search Chair. Carl was a lawyer by training with a business leadership pedigree of which most executives can only dream. Over lunch he demonstrated his aptitude at asking probing questions and gently following up on them to get at the heart of the matter, an incredibly important attribute for a Search Chair. The ability to ask the right questions and dig out information without appearing too obvious is a learned skill.

So at lunch I asked Carl if he'd be the Search Chair. Fred, Carl, and the other two board members quickly discussed among themselves before Carl asked me what was involved. I gave him a general overview, and he agreed. I think he was more than happy to keep an eye on what he probably considered a young pup, because he's got at least two and a half decades on me.

Normally we could have completed everything we needed that day on-site, but in this case the manufacturing facility where the COO was to be located was in Milwaukee, Wisconsin. Before we left that day, we made arrangements to tour the facility with Fred and Carl. It is absolutely critical that as a recruiter you see the hire's proposed working environment if it's not local. You can't assume the company culture is consistent across multiple facilities if they're more than a half-day's drive away.

Michael and I returned to our hotel, unpacked, had dinner, combined our notes, and prepared to head back home.

How to Form a Functional Search Committee

After a combined 45 years of recruiting we can guarantee one thing: On the client side, managing an executive search project is a full-time job.

Generally speaking, boards of directors rarely have the requisite experience, detailed operational knowledge, and, more importantly, the time to commit 100 percent of their effort to recruiting an executive—crucial though that may be. Most board members are unaware of the amount of time that's required up front—and throughout the process—to locate, court, and win over great candidates. This isn't a part-time activity. It's simply too time intensive and critical to the organization's success. So the first step the board should take is to appoint a Search Committee to oversee the project, no different from establishing an audit committee.

When selecting a Search Committee, you should carefully weigh the answers to these five questions:

1. Which outside board members have been successful CEOs in their respective careers?

2. Who is best positioned to invest the appropriate time into the process?

3. Who is in the best position to evaluate and *persuade* candidates?

4. You may want to have peer level executives on the Search Committee: Just make sure there are no conflicting agendas, or you risk being sabotaged.

5. Who has successfully conducted CEO- or executive-level searches in the recent past? This is a key issue. If no one on your board has the experience, consider bringing someone in from the outside who has. (*Success should have a heavy weighting toward exit and shareholder value and not just who got a bargain on entry compensation.*)

*NOTE: Keep the Search Committee small. Five to seven committed peo-
ple is ideal. That is small enough to have animated discussions while large
enough not to be swayed by one person.*

It's important to recognize both the public and private reasons
behind the search, discuss the overall parameters of the strategy,
and agree on the charter and deliverables of the Search Committee.
Depending on the circumstances, the current CEO may or may not be
a part of this committee. There are pros and cons to both: Consider
what may be most appropriate if you need help closing on your most
desired candidate.

The charter of the Search Committee is straightforward:

- Confirm the real needs.

- Create a critical path and/or timeline for the complete end-
  to-end recruitment and hiring process.

- Build board consensus on strategy and agenda.

- Help create a detailed, competency-based job description that
  realistically defines the role, critical skills, and experience *and*
  ties it to the business plan. (This is the one activity that the
  chair must get right or you will fail BUT for random luck.)

- Ensure the legal requirements for due diligence are met.

- Manage the candidate selection and search process.

- Land the best candidate.

Next, we're going to select a Search Committee chairperson.

How to Select a Search Committee Chairperson

The Search Committee should appoint a chair during its first meeting.
Who should you choose? While evaluating the potential chair, it will
become apparent who has the relevant experience, as well as the time
and interest to invest in the project. It's highly recommended that the
chair of the Search Committee be an outside board member detached
from the organization's internal politics.

The chair is responsible for leading open discussions, promoting honest communications, and gaining member commitment and consensus with the goal of bringing new talent and expertise to an organization. More challenging and equally important, the chair must be able to develop personal relationships with candidates. This is critical in the closing process. And above all, the chair needs to be extremely accessible and proactive in the pursuit of candidates throughout the entire search process.

The correct Search Committee chair is vital to the ultimate success of the search. He or she keeps everyone and everything moving forward by leading the process and guiding decisions. The chair must allow everyone on the committee to be heard without letting dissenters and detractors hijack the group. The chair's major challenge is to gain consensus from the group, remembering that you can't always please everyone all the time. A successful search is dependent on a myriad of variables that the chair must manage, while ensuring the following basic components are in place with the ESP before the search begins:

- A detailed process.

- Realistic expectations on timing and costs clearly defined.

- A concise and descriptive timeline.

- A competency-based profile of the ideal candidate based on KPIs the executive to be hired will be assessed against.

- A rigorous sourcing and recruiting process.

- An organized and coordinated interview and final selection process.

The Search Chair should also appoint an internal coordinator to work with the committee. This coordinator is responsible for managing the calendars of the participants, interview logistics, and feedback loops. On a daily basis the coordinator ensures all elements of the search process remain on track, while also being the vault and central repository of all documentation and reports sent by the ESP. I've found the Search Chair's most trusted executive assistant works best for everyone, because he or she likely already has a working relationship with the board members and can get to them quickly.

DUTIES OF THE SEARCH COMMITTEE CHAIRPERSON

- Build an emotional link with the right candidate (*this is absolutely crucial*).

- Work with the ESP—help create and manage an appropriate timeline.

- Serve as the "voice" for the Search Committee in the creation of position profiles.

- Drive the process with the search firm.

- Manage information flow between the Search Committee and board.

- Help the ESP gather data about recommended candidates from all board members and "friends" of the company.

- Evaluate and manage any internal candidates with the ESP.

- Drive the creation, development, and presentation of the appropriate offer.

- Play "good cop" if the ESP needs to step aside in the negotiation phase.

- Be personally involved in checking references, ensuring due diligence, negotiating the offer, and closing the candidate.

- In the final analysis the Search Chair is often in the best position to convince the candidate there's a fit and articulate why his or her backgrounds/skills/opportunities/challenges align, along with explaining why there's wealth to be made. This last point is critical—especially for funded ventures. Cap structures are often complex and it's hard for a newcomer to anticipate how much additional funding will be required, and in how many tranches. Only the Search Chair can see and tell this story.

Bringing a new senior executive into your company implies change, and change, when managed well, creates opportunity. The attention you give to a search project, and your interactions with your ESP and candidates, provides the foundation for success. If *you both* work at the process together, the probability of attracting your ideal candidate is almost assured.

Let me illustrate what we mean by this. One task of the Search Chair is to make the best use of the points of contact a company has with the ESP and candidates. Even the best opportunities—much like the best investments—don't sell themselves automatically to the best candidates. They need to be explained. It's the consultant who breathes life into your opportunity and makes it real and desirable for prospects. The keys to maximizing your results follow.

How to Manage the Process

Be in the moment and fully engaged whenever you're speaking with the ESP and candidates. This is the number one rule for success. Show your interest, stay involved, and actively manage and participate in the search. Your subordinates need to see your stamp of approval on the search, so they appreciate the value of its success. Engage your top management team. Where advisable, seek their opinions. Confirm their buy-in. Let them know what it is you want the new executive to accomplish, then make the search a priority on your agenda. Make it absolutely clear you want the search to succeed and your new person to be brought on board. Make your schedule available to the ESP and candidates.

Expect Greatness

Be realistic in your expectations about the time required to find and screen appropriate candidates and determine compensation, but expect your search to produce high quality candidates. In turn, the ESP should be realistic with you. If their promises are too glowing, be wary. "Chemistry," for example, is the leading reason candidates are rejected. You should insist on a *Benchmark Interview* with a candidate the ESP deems close to your requirements, if they know anyone. This benchmarking exercise will give you and the ESP critical insight about the chemistry being sought.

Be Ruthless

You have a right to know what's going on, so be inquisitive. Ask the ESP about their search strategy, status, problems, market feedback, and other elements of the search. Monitor their progress. *Require* the ESP to speak with you directly by phone every week to ten days so you stay on top of the project. If the search runs into a strong headwind, ask to talk with them twice a week.

Be Paranoid

Thoroughly check out the finalist before an offer is extended. Contact some (or all) of the references *yourself. We have found that executives are less apt to lie to business peers.* (There is no harm in having two people call the same reference, especially if something isn't clear. More on this later in the chapter on referencing.) In this day and age of extreme makeovers, it's wise to be prudently skeptical lest you find someone has put lipstick on a pig. As Andy Groove said, "Only the paranoid survive." A hiring mistake at this level is not easy to fix and may cause a great deal of harm before it's discovered.

Your Rapport with the Executive Search Professional

It's your company, so let the ESP know how you like to operate and your expectations. The best ones are flexible and will work to match your style. Treat them as you would your best staff. Openly communicate your company's situation, needs, problems, and objectives. Make the search a partnership. Communicate an attitude of trust and teamwork and listen to your consultant with an open mind. You may disagree with their advice, but their experience can save you a lot of time and trouble. (Remember: Executive search is as much an art as it is a science. So if your consultant has a gut level feeling about an issue, you'd be wise to listen carefully.)

Let the ESP evaluate candidates identified through internal sources and candidates just as they would those found through their own sources. Above all, openly discuss your selection biases and the qualities that just don't work in your company—and there *will* be some. Ask the ESP what their biases are, too. (For example, political animals drive me nuts, and I need to ignore my bias in most cases.)

Question the ESP on the "whys" behind their conclusions. Why are the people presented as final candidates? How closely does each candidate meet the most important criteria? What has each candidate really accomplished? What does the ESP see as potential problem areas with each candidate? What has the ESP learned from references?

If you sense problems during the search, be open and candid with the ESP. Create a problem-solving environment. This is what I meant by the "we're all in this together" attitude I mentioned earlier, which can be a strong motivation for the consultant. Finger-pointing may kill their incentive to work hard on your behalf.

Confer at predetermined intervals on whether the job specifications have changed, or priorities have been reordered. Rarely is a spec static throughout a search. It's always a work in progress, and it's natural to reorder skills and experience on the fly.

But above all, being accessible is the simplest and most effective way of demonstrating your commitment to the search's success. The vast majority of interactions with candidates happen after the dinner hour when most nine-to-fivers are watching TV or reading bedtime stories to their children. Exchange home telephone numbers. Introduce your administrative assistant. And keep the ESP in the know regarding major blocks of time when you'll be unavailable, like board meetings and vacations. Being both up-front and accessible demonstrates how serious you are about the process, which in turn inspires the ESP's confidence in you and your firm, leading to a more effective search overall.

CHAPTER 3

Preparation

RecruiterNomics

The greatest victory is that which requires no battle.
　　　　　　　　　　—Sun Tzu, *The Art of War*

V ital to the success of every executive hire is a crystal-clear under-standing of the roles and responsibilities of the job, as well as the physical work environment in which the job will be fulfilled. While Michael and I were there primarily to vet the job description we'd been provided with, line-by-line, we also wanted to tour the plant and meet some of the staff as we had in Los Angeles. It's absolutely critical to thoroughly understand the opportunity you're selling if you want to attract the best people, because candidates are tired of being "pitched."

The visit to Milwaukee did not disappoint us. It was clear Fred ran a tight ship. The buildings, from the factory floor to executive offices, were neat and tidy, clean and well organized. Touring the factory floor with Fred was a real lesson in employee engagement. Fred stopped and spoke with dozens of employees we crossed paths with. He was sincere and interested in what was happening in their lives—inquiring about little Suzie's softball game or John's college graduation. Little wonder the plant's turnover was near zero and they had a long list of people waiting to join as older workers began to retire.

It was clear to us that whomever we recruited would have very large shoes to fill. Not only did they need to understand the machin-ery as well as Fred, but would also need to be as approachable and as personable. We concluded the Milwaukee plant would show well. We could almost guarantee that all the potential candidates we con-tacted and brought forward in the search would be curious enough to do a drive-by and inspect the plant's exterior before saying "yes" to a meeting. They would only be encouraged to proceed.

Michael said we should ask potential candidates if they had driven by the facility as a qualifier while doing phone screens. Great idea, I thought. It made sense that anyone who hadn't done at least that much before speaking with us after receiving the position profile and CCB could be running away from something, rather than being drawn toward a more positive opportunity. It was a red flag to watch for.

I was convinced Fred's opportunity would be strongly coveted. The job description Fred had given us was spot-on. He'd put a lot of thought into it, and it was accurate. From that moment, we knew for sure the reason the search failed the first two times was the hands-off restrictions of the other two firms. Fred's a smart businessman. If he'd been made aware of this potentially limiting factor I'm certain he would have contracted a boutique search firm, and we never would've met. Lucky for us!

During both our visits with Fred in Los Angeles and then Milwaukee, we were impressed. We were learning more about him, his company and the position we'd been contacted about, and as we again picked apart the job description line-by-line, things just kept getting better. But we were just beginning our learning process. We needed to keep hammering away at that job description. Because clearly defining the executive's role and responsibilities in relation to the entire executive team, and detailing their contribution to the business, is critical to the long-term success of the new hire. As an ESP, candidates will ask you umpteen details about the company and the role.

And if you can't answer, you're dead.

THE IMPORTANCE OF DUE DILIGENCE

Here's a quick story illustrating why a proper job description is crucial to your ultimate success, and why not doing so may lead to unrealized ambitions.

Several years ago a friend of mine, Brian, joined a 40-person, five-year-old start-up (AMESS) as a vice-president of sales. Toward the end of his second month in this new position he invited me to visit to the new company to discuss recruitment, at the request of the CEO. Brian introduced me to the CEO with great fanfare and then excused himself. I turned my attention to the CEO to say something when he said, "I want you to find me a replacement for Brian. He's not working out."

Apparently, after just two months, Brian was a huge disappointment.

I sat down, more than a little stunned and keeping a straight face as the CEO explained, in great detail, the pain and suffering they had experienced staffing the role. The CEO spoke for several hours, interspersing his monologue with quotes from *Crossing the Chasm* and *Good to Great*.

It quickly became quite clear, at least to me, that his dissatisfaction with Brian was evidence of more systemic issues. I say this first because the CEO was having difficulty hiring in several areas of the company and, second, because Brian was the fifth VP of sales in just two years.

I became intensely curious as to the process his firm used to hire talent: how they identified roles, and how to fill them. "Fuzzy" is the best way to describe it. Led by the CEO, he and the board described the role in one sentence as "responsible for all sales and marketing." I clearly remember thinking, "that's not very helpful." Here was a perfect opportunity to leverage his human resource person, but he decided they weren't likely to recognize talent if they "tripped over it." That's a direct quote, by the way. Such disdain for the HR manager was neither smart nor healthy, from a business standpoint. HR professionals are trained in exactly this—and can usually get into the minutiae of a role better than anyone. The CEO just needed to let the HR person at it, I thought.

The cavalier attitude the CEO displayed with his job description was surpassed only by the lack of thought directed at how best to identify, qualify, and recruit the sales leader they were looking for. Oh sure, I learned, the investors and board members had made several suggestions for likely candidates whom they knew to be solid and who were leading a very successful competitor. But no up-front work to define the skills, connections, and technical knowledge required to excel at the job had been done.

As the CEO described it, many months passed waiting for a response to their ad with nothing to show for it. Later, after they hired a recruiter to find the right person, again nothing. When they did finally interview several candidates, the board disagreed on whom to hire. As time ran out, they settled on a compromise selection that left everyone dissatisfied. There was no broad consensus. Unfortunately, the compromise's performance lagged and the inevitable firing took place. Each time, the obligatory post-mortem found the candidate's experience to be lacking, but they failed to determine how. They simply dismissed it as bad luck.

To my surprise, not once did the CEO or board pause to consider why the wrong person was selected in the first place. I found an excuse not to accept any of their search work and Brian was recruited away several months later, to a company where he remains nine years later. Between

1995 and 2011, AMESS cycled through 11 VPs of sales and its sales barely budged. AMESS was later acquired by a startup for its technology. Ironically, the business press held the CEO up as a shining example of perseverance. Personally, I know his investors were NOT celebrating.

As an aside, I need to tell you that previously I had recruited Brian. He had had a consistent 20-year history of success. Since leaving AMESS, Brian has "fixed" and sold two other companies—returning huge value to the shareholders.

Was that story familiar to you? If so, I'm sorry. Most hiring is done ready-fire-aim. Is there a better way? You bet!

A successful executive search begins with a thorough and formal definition of roles, responsibilities, and competencies. Once this is determined, the personal and the professional attributes necessary for success are overlaid onto the cultural and environmental factors distinct to the organization. Every event and decision made in the recruiting process must be derived from the corporate strategy, which drives the job description, which influences the essential candidate characteristics. AMESS repeatedly failed in its recruiting efforts because senior management didn't take the time to properly define its true needs and objectives.

What? You say you've heard all this before, and, even though you've honestly tried to apply these concepts, you still haven't succeeded in hiring the right executives? Process by itself doesn't guarantee you'll end up with a quality search, but it starts there. But without a logical process, you're placing your bottom line in the hands of lady luck that you'll attract and hire that mythical star candidate.

So let me ask you right now, just between us: How thorough is your process and do you follow it? If you're like 98 percent of the CEOs and hiring managers we've met over the past three decades, you'll get some of it right. But in today's hypercompetitive business environment you no longer have the luxury of winging it, or trying someone for six months to see if they'll work out. No, recruiting executive talent is not something you want to try learning on the fly when the situation arises. You either get it right the first time, or not. Screw it up and the best thing that can happen is that no one talks to you. On the other hand, the worst thing that can happen is your competitors harvest the best talent while you get crushed.

Hiring Greatness

Figure 3.1   Foundation Documents.

What follows is a deceptively simple, rock solid, and effective way to establish a firm foundation for your executive search project, which starts with defining the role—precisely.

THE JOB DESCRIPTION—YOUR FOUNDATIONAL DOCUMENT

If this is the first time you've needed to write this role's job description and don't have a vice-president of human resources or chief talent officer at your disposal, then may we suggest you first consult Google. Seriously, so many job descriptions (Figure 3.1) are available on the Internet you don't need to suffer through creating one from scratch. Simply visit Google and type in the position title, which changes of course for each job, and your industry. If you look at the example below, I found 146,000 results in less than a second. Your results will be different but we're certain you get the idea. Keeping with our example, if Fred was Google searching he'd type in "chief operating officer"—"manufacturing" (see Figure 3.2).

Your job description is a foundational document. Everything else in the search will spring from it. Before you develop a position profile, assess the marketplace, and research target companies—let alone begin to recruit—you must first have a clear picture of the role and what's required for success.

Google   job description "chief operating officer" "manufacturing"   🔍

Web   News   Images   Videos   More ▾   Search tools

About 146,000 results (0.52 seconds)

Figure 3.2   Google search for chief operating officer job descriptions.

You first need to determine who needs to be involved in defining the role and its outcomes. While this sounds like common sense, if
you ask too many people you run the risk of developing a spec that fits
everyone's needs a little. This leads to compromise, and a weak job
description that aimlessly satisfies everyone *but* doesn't get at the meat
of the role. Compromise is a bad idea. You need to get at the specifics
of the role quickly and then succinctly detail them on paper. So, as the
executive role warrants—and on a situation-by-situation basis—you
should involve your board of directors, any senior executives directly
affected by the position, and, on rare occasions, peers and subordinates
(very, very rare occasions).

To begin, choose either an impartial board member or outside
facilitator to lead the group through the exercise of describing the
job's content, objectives, performance measures, essential technical
and management skills, and—most importantly—fit.

Deconstruct the role's responsibilities based on your organization's business plan in light of its past, present, and future needs. Then
reconstruct the role from the ground up to reflect what you need today
(as opposed to yesterday), accounting for skills, experience, and other
essentials that may be required two to three years out.

Next you need to recognize, acknowledge, and account for the
specific challenges that may be unique to your industry. Successful
recruiting necessitates understanding exactly where your company is
in its evolution from start-up to multinational, how fast it's changing,
and what the current and future skills gap looks like (Figure 3.3).
Moreover, you need to decide on the appropriateness of your current
team's skills mix, and how the new position will impact other roles and
even bolster weaknesses in other areas of your management team.

Beware, the entire world *does not* move at Google speed, so
be careful what job description(s) you model yours after because it

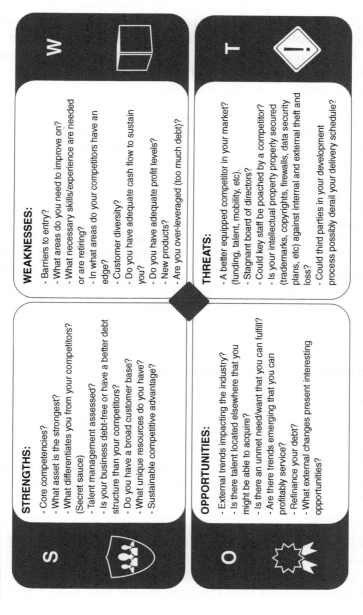

SWOT ANALYSIS

STRENGTHS:
- Core competencies?
- What asset is the strongest?
- What differentiates you from your competitors? (Secret sauce)
- Talent management assessed?
- Is your business debt-free or have a better debt structure than your competitors?
- Do you have a broad customer base?
- What unique resources do you have?
- Sustainable competitive advantage?

WEAKNESSES:
- Barriers to entry?
- What areas do you need to improve on?
- What necessary skills/experience are needed or are retiring?
- In what areas do your competitors have an edge?
- Customer diversity?
- Do you have adequate cash flow to sustain you?
- Do you have adequate profit levels?
- New products?
- Are you over-leveraged (too much debt)?

OPPORTUNITIES:
- External trends impacting the industry?
- Is there talent located elsewhere that you might be able to acquire?
- Is there an unmet need/want that you can fulfill?
- Are there trends emerging that you can profitably service?
- Refinance your debt?
- What external changes present interesting opportunities?

THREATS:
- A better equipped competitor in your market? (funding, talent, mobility, etc).
- Stagnant board of directors?
- Could key staff be poached by a competitor?
- Is your intellectual property properly secured (trademarks, copyrights, firewalls, data security plans, etc) against internal and external theft and loss?
- Could third parties in your development process possibly derail your delivery schedule?

Figure 3.3 SWOT analysis of the current state of the business used to build the job description.

45

might sound sexy—but be entirely inappropriate for your needs. The high-tech industry is very different from other industries in terms of its rapid pace of change. Yes, technology affects other industries. But it's the high-tech industry that makes the technology that affects everyone, so they usually feel the effects of innovation first and often years ahead of the general market. For example, disruptive companies like Google, Uber, Alibaba, or Airbnb can experience explosive growth, while the company down the street may struggle to survive for years. Both likely require a different mix of skills and experiences.

As an example, the right chief operating officer for a mid-sized manufacturing company will be different from the one you'd hire for a $100 million company looking to double revenue over the next 24 months, or a multinational looking to expand into Asia this year.

The customers, business cycle, and value proposition for each will look drastically different, yet both need an experienced COO to succeed. It's wishful thinking that any successful COO could necessarily thrive in the other's environment. The first company from the above example needs a supportive, "coach"-like COO; the second most likely needs a battle-hardened "field general;" and the last a "diplomat" able to deal with foreign dignitaries. That's not to say you can't find the rare individual who's experienced in all three, but it's unlikely.

To Master the Basics—Start Here

The basics of a solid job description include title, to whom the position reports (in the case of Tulip, it's the CEO/owner and board of directors), a summary of the position, the specific functional requirement for the job, and the education and specific experience necessary to fulfill the role. Whenever it's possible to detail the organizational reporting structure you should do so, but keep in mind this information will almost certainly fall into the hands of a competitor—so err conservatively.

The job description is the tool you need in order to craft your position profile (PP), which is for public consumption. And even if you choose not to include these in the job description, detail the accomplishments your ideal candidate should have to be a perfect fit.

You'll use that information when you construct the PP. Remember: you're not only searching for someone with the correct education, impeccable qualifications, and who would be a good fit with the organization, but also someone with a verifiable track record of success in the role.

Because a COO's role can vary from company to company you must assess which departments in your organization the COO should oversee, be it all or just a few. The same can be said for every other executive role. At a minimum, though, no matter what stage of growth the company is at, you need to appraise the following.

Responsibility

- Start with your goal in mind, which must be agreed upon by everyone involved in the hire. Disagreement will be flagged by an intuitive candidate and may sideswipe your hiring initiative.

- What does the business plan call for from this role? Exactly what results are you looking for the new executive to produce? Build the business? Turn it around? Flip it? Modernize it? Stabilize it? Talk through the job's expectation at length with your goal in mind. Don't be in the least bit fuzzy.

- Lay out the specific activities involved.

- Is it a new job or an existing one? Stay specific. Detail where there's overlap with other executive functions and determine who owns what.

- What are the contact points with other positions?

- Does the role require the hire to carry on with an established foundation, or start from scratch?

Leadership

- What is the role's predominant or preferred style of leadership? (By the way, leadership is situational as companies are in constant flux—now more than ever. However, most people have a preferred/dominant leadership style. What style does

the role call for now, along with three to five years from now?
Best to know what you need before you go any further.)

Authority

- Draw up the org chart. This is not for public consumption, but
  will help determine the touch points throughout the company
  and flush out any considerations that need to be weighed. For
  example: In some cases the COO handles HR directly, but the
  VP of sales may have recruiting reporting to them. You need
  to account for that in the role.

- Also, spell out the informal networks that keep the organization humming. Who's on the side? Who's not? (This is
  especially important with a family-run business.)

- Which departments are strong and which are weak? Where
  does the company need to add bench strength?

Performance Requirements

- Establish and agree upon *observable* and *measurable* performance requirements. You should start your relationship with
  all new hires with observable and measurable requirements
  in place. Due to the fact that observable and measureable
  performance standards are purely objective, not only will you
  know where the new hire stands but *so will they* when it comes
  time for the yearly review without prejudice.

- Codify the hard skills needed for the job.

- Soft skills.

- What's more important in the role today: industry knowledge
  or industry contacts?

- List experience requirements in detail.

- Must candidates possess experience in your industry? To what
  degree must they have already been in a comparable role
  elsewhere?

- What specific experiences are absolute must-haves versus nice-to-haves? Make sure you spell them out and document it so this is clear to everyone involved in the hire.

- Also list execution parameters that are flexible and those that are not.

Personal Qualities

- Define the essential personal qualities required for the role.

- Consider the environment, culture, and personal styles that work best in your organization. Do you want more of the same?

- Decide the degree to which a compatible style is of importance. Are you looking for a change agent? (Actually, "change agent" is an overused, misunderstood, and misinterpreted term, so scrub it from your job description or fully define it.)

- Do you want a person who will be counter to the established company culture or someone who will promote it?

Fit—How Well This Candidate's Personality and Management Style Mesh with Superiors, Peers, and Subordinates

- Reflect on who succeeds and who doesn't in your company. Why do people leave?

- What is the management style of this person's future boss?

- What styles won't work with their future boss?

- If the job requires a high degree of contact with customers and outsiders, think through the image and approach that work best in your market space.

List of compensation issues.

Compensation—For a Complete List of Compensation Issues Consult the Website for a Free Download

- Specify all elements of the compensation package.

- Gather objective, competitive market data.

- Think about the upper limits of compensation. If the absolutely perfect candidate came along, how far are you prepared to stretch—if at all?

- Besides base salary, what do people in your company receive and what do they value?

- Will you pay relocation costs?

- Is relocation absolutely necessary?

Also, consider whether you want to allow some flexibility in hiring based on the strengths of your best candidates. At the end of this process, you and the Search Committee should have a crystal-clear job description complete with roles, responsibilities, authority, and desired qualifications.

In constructing a job description, is there necessarily one right way? Is there magic involved in finding talented executives? The answer to both of these questions, of course, is, "No." There is no one way. The secret to long-lasting results rests in the hard work, good judgment, follow-up, and attention to detail on the part of everyone involved. It's a meticulously detailed process, which needs to be executed with the highest degree of skill and precision. This starts with your job description.

The degree of specificity and clarity required in the language of the job description is absolutely essential to a successful recruiting process. I honed the ability to draft succinct job descriptions while brainstorming for over three years on task force committees for the Society for Human Resource Management (SHRM), developing ANSI and ISO human resource standards. I can attest there's a lot of language used in job descriptions that gets left open for misinterpretation.

The need for clarifying job descriptions through standardization throughout the recruiting industry is recognized by Lee Webster, who notes that:

> The current act of developing, presenting, and applying job descriptions has become overburdened with jargon laden content and effuse language that obscures rather than reveals the nature of the work. Through standardization, job descriptions would become nimble documents, specifying the capabilities needed by employers to accomplish their organizational goals.
>
> **—Lee Webster, JD-MBA, SPHR, GPHR,**
> **Director, Talent Acquisition and Recruitment,**
> **University of Texas Medical Branch**

CREATING THE POSITION PROFILE

Start your position profile by thinking about WIFM. No, this is not an FM radio station.

At this point in the process it's really all about the candidate. After all, you don't get to choose who you want to work for you unless they're interested first. The greatest frustration in recruiting executives is that, unlike traditional capital, *human capital* has a voice in the outcome. And highly sought-after executives use their voice to great effect. No matter how attractive they may be to you, they can—and often do—say, "No!"

Your first mission, then, is to understand their WIFM Factor: *What's in It for Me?*

Drive to Own the "Means of Employment"

We're currently riding a great historical trend: the compelling need everyone feels for control over their own fate. People are taking control of their lives, and this means ownership of the *means of employment.* The mere thought that people might actually want to control their own destiny would befuddle Henry Ford to no end. But taking control of one's employment is especially important in today's demographic, because so many people are looking for new kinds of work—work that has meaning for them. Our population is getting older—for the first time, there will soon be more people over 65 than under five— and older people are more reflective. They want to know they're doing something meaningful.

> "Why is it every time I ask for a pair of hands, they come with a brain attached?"
> —Henry Ford

Some 87 percent of the 140 million working Americans want a different job. This costs the country trillions of dollars in foregone productivity. Gallup research shows that in the United States, more than half of employees are not engaged at work—and 20 percent are actively disengaged.[1] The cost of all this disengagement in lost productivity is about $300 billion a year. This can only be solved at the most basic level; each individual has to find his or her own specific road to job satisfaction, and that requires individual ownership of the means of employment!

The nature of work is also changing as people seek control. A new business model for the twenty-first century is arising. Enjoyment-based motivation, namely how creative a person feels when working on the project, is the strongest and most pervasive drive for many workers today. Control over your work leads to the pure joy of creating. As the economy moves toward more right-brained conceptual work, the motivators presented to those stressing self-satisfaction and self-motivation must also change.

More and more people are working to their own tune: 15 million people telecommute every day, which is a large part of the workforce beyond the gaze of a manager. Employers therefore need to adjust their tactics to get the attention of high performance people. Organizations also need to hire leaders who "get it" and can engage employees to bring their A-game to work every day, because employees typically don't quit companies—they quit bosses.

What's in It for Me?

So before you risk losing your next great prospect, take your boring job description and breathe life into it so the potential executive you approach understands the depth of the opportunity and is at least curious to learn more. That's where the marketing comes in. You may have noticed that all cars have four wheels, seats, and an engine. With some differences, arguably all cars are the same: Ultimately they're designed to take you from point A to point B. Yet they sell at different price points, and some are so coveted they have waiting lists years long just to test-drive them. It's great marketing that will create the same type of longing for your job opening.

Here's how to do that. Keep in mind that your cleverly crafted position profile (PP) may be considered what Seth Godin calls "interruption marketing" in his book *Permission Marketing: Turning Strangers into Friends and Friends Into Customers* (New York: Simon & Schuster, 1999). You don't start by asking them to interview for your job on first contact. You earn the right, over time, bit by bit.[2]

To attract the best talent, your job description should market your company as a great place to work. It must be appealing, attractive, as brief as possible without leaving out the essentials, and true to your brand. Make no mistake, you have a brand—whether you consciously created it or not—and you can bet that if your potential candidate doesn't look online to see what people are saying about you, someone in their family may. To better understand the implications we invite you to download the supplementary piece on "Branding for Executive Attraction" by Rayanne Thorn, from this book's website. In this case the job description should start with a tightly worded yet interesting overview of the opportunity, one that piques the prospect's curiosity and either qualifies or disqualifies them from consideration straight off. We've found that if you do your research correctly and reach out to a carefully targeted list of people, you'll be speaking to qualified candidates more than 99 percent of the time.

More specifically, in five to seven pages, the position profile includes:

1. A cover page with the title of the role and your logo clearly displayed on it, preferably with an attention-grabbing graphic that conveys the essence of the company or the role.

2. On the first page, an opening statement of no more than five to seven paragraphs describing the company, its product or services, mission, and vision. It positions the company within your industry and, above all else, creates curiosity. This is a tall order for most people and we suggest you allow marketing experts help with this. Other useful details might include stats such as number of employees, annual sales, industry accolades, and so on.

3. Details about the role. With the job description you just created in hand, write a brief description of the position and its
   major responsibilities or goals. Keep it short and to the point
   and focused on outcomes for the role. Candidates need to
   understand how their contribution will be measured and what
   constitutes success in absolute terms. So tell them.

   • Title, roles, and responsibilities and what they'll be doing
     (objectives). Whenever practical, include details on who
     the person's peers are and the org chart for the depart-
     ment or division. Alternatively, you may want to keep this
     hidden from prying eyes until you're down to your final
     selection. Let the candidate ask questions about it in the
     interview but understand ahead of time what you need to
     guard as confidential in case you do *not* bring this individ-
     ual forward.

   • Any specialized knowledge, skills, or abilities. List all
     qualifications that are absolutely mandatory, along with
     those that are preferred. Your list of qualifications should
     include specific skills, years of experience, certifications,
     licenses, education level (though this is less and less an
     issue with senior executives), and necessary technical
     proficiencies. The laundry list of skills often present in
     cleverly written job postings found on job boards are
     designed to cast a wide net—exactly what you *don't* want.
     These catchall descriptions do more harm than good,
     and your preferred candidates will deem you "light."

As an example, we specified these deliverables in the position profile for a vice-president of customer engagement:

Specific deliverables for year one:

Complete the rollout of the Satmetrix customer care systems after
   operationalizing a regional hub-and-spoke model

In keeping with the CEO's "strategic vision," innovate and enhance
   the survey process and design of the system to achieve the
   company's revenue goals by aligning the NPS system/tool with
   other initiatives and systems

Decentralize the system and embolden others to use the tool to
   enhance their business units

1. Our Ideal Candidate: This is a concise description that blends the ideal hard and soft skills you believe will work best for success in the role. The section may run a full page and needs to cover accomplishments and previous responsibilities. Its purpose is to make the reader understand why he or she is qualified *and* "see" him- or herself in the role.

   - *Qualifications and Core Competencies*—The picture you paint about the ideal candidate should be desirable, and includes a bit of "stretch" to help pitch the role as something they would consider the next step in their career.

   - *Your Personality Characteristics*—Consider a candidate's behavioral and personality traits, as well as soft skills like communication, work ethic, attitude, and values. "Fit" is the most subjective part of any hire and is most often sighted as a reason for terminating a new hire. Why jeopardize months of work and potentially millions of dollars in lost opportunity costs by hiring someone who just doesn't work well with your team? Take time now to explain or characterize the type of people who succeed at your organization. This allows prospective executives the opportunity to screen themselves in or out from the start.

2. Next Steps: This is a brief explanation on how to proceed.

   - Be careful here. If you execute correctly on your search, most people you contact will come through research efforts (later in this chapter) and those people are likely to be fully employed and happy where they are. These types of people usually decline the first offer immediately because they'd rather have a root canal than write a résumé, so invite them to have a conversation first without the need for a résumé. The additional benefit to this is you'll discover what's most important to them during your first meeting or call. The questions people ask at this juncture are very revealing. They'll be relaxed and "real," perhaps quite unlike their persona during a formal interview.

   - Detailed contact points to move forward are essential, so spell out with dedicated phone numbers and a personal email address how and when are the best time(s) to get hold of you or the ESP responsible.

3. Frequently Asked Questions: The final section is optional. This is the perfect place to explain compensation if you choose to use it as a filter. If you haven't hyperlinked them in your document this is where you may provide links to your website, company newsletter, annual report, and 10-K. Think hard about anything else you'd personally want to know or research at this early stage before you made a multimillion-dollar investment in a company. Five items are plenty.

Creating a candidate profile helps define a full, accurate picture of the ideal candidate. In the end you'll truly *"know them when you see them,"* because you understand the type of person you need before you start interviewing. Please see Appendix A for the position profile used for the COO search we created for Tulip or download it from the book's website at www.HiringGreatness.com.

Position profile for Tulip COO search.

Formatting Tips

The perfect PP is neither too descriptive nor too vague, uses clear language, and represents the ethos of the company. Here are a few formatting tips for improving your company's job descriptions:

- **Bullet point when possible:** As you did with your job description, make your PP easy to read by using bullet points within the responsibilities and qualifications sections and anywhere else that makes sense.

- **Be specific:** While brevity is a much appreciated art, it's also important to be as specific and transparent as possible in your job description. Vague descriptions make it difficult for potential applicants to imagine themselves in a role and decide whether they're qualified for or would enjoy the job.

- **Use direct language:** It's important to give potential applicants a clear idea of the responsibilities and qualifications necessary for the job. Organize the responsibilities and the desired qualifications by degree of importance to the role's expected level of success. Most people will automatically assume the first line they read is the most important, the second line the next most important, and so on. Use this to your advantage, especially if the bulleted lists run more than five items: They won't all have equal importance, and you need to make that clear or applicants will draw their own conclusions.

- **Embody the company's character:** When crafting your PP choose a writing style and words that match your company's culture. If your business is a start-up with a very distinct ethos, be sure to communicate that sentiment with the way you format your description, the words you use, and general feelings your writing evokes. If that means straying from the norm, so be it. In the end, the goal is to attract people who are right for the position and the company.

While it's true that any new employee needs to be part of the long-term corporate strategy, it's especially true when hiring a new executive. Outlining the specific accomplishments your ideal candidate should have on the PP will keep everyone in the interview process on the same track. Remember you're not only searching for someone with the requisite education, qualifications, and personal fit but also with a proven track record of success within the defined role.

THE CONFIDENTIAL CANDIDATE BRIEF

Remember, we're concerned with attracting candidates with the *right stuff*—the best candidates, not the ones trolling the job boards or who would respond to that poorly disguised phone call from a recruiter: "Do you know of anyone who is interested in this position?" That's for hiring the inexperienced. The true movers and shakers who drive your industry are the real prize. "Passive candidate" is the label best used to describe them.

How to Get People to Stick Their Hands Up and Self-Select

Early in my career as a headhunter, and decades before teaming up with Mark Haluska, I made a name for myself within the executive search industry by batting cleanup for name brand multinational search firms where a search project had gone off the rails. I had the good fortune of being asked by a very senior ESP, who had taken on too much work, to recontact potential candidates who had said no when he'd first contacted them. It turns out that I was good at turning NOs into conversations, and I developed this skill into a thriving part of my practice. "Resurrecting the dead" was what one search client called it.

For more than a decade in the late 1980s and 1990s, I was *the guy* search firms called when they needed to speak with a potential candidate who was continuously ducking their calls. As it turned out, I was good at getting people to say "yes." My secret at the time was how I researched the passive candidate before picking up the phone.

Turns out, a little common sense research brings huge benefits. Those executives regarded most recruiters as pests who wanted something from them—the bounty on their head. Like the recruiters who had tried unsuccessfully to call them, I was an outsider, a stranger. They were correct in their thinking: I really had no right to talk to them. So what did we have in common? What value could I possibly bring to their life? When you figure that out, it's easy to start a conversation. And it's not that hard to figure out.

If you want to understand someone without their cooperation, you need to find people who know them and who will talk to you. Networking with the recently departed became a staple in my arsenal. Trouble is, the best candidates are usually being aggressively shielded by their employers and away from recruiters. Cloaked by call screening, e-mail filters, and ever-more-watchful HR departments, it's more difficult than ever to pry them free—assuming you can find them.

This type of arduous spadework was simplified with the advent of Google, online résumés, and newsgroup gatherings. The process was further accelerated by a company called Eliyon Technologies, now named ZoomInfo. It was ZoomInfo that automated a lot of this tedious research by making it blazingly quick to find nearly any executive I wanted to reach. ZoomInfo's database boasts over 138 million profiles of business professionals, with 8.5 million company profiles that can be searched by name, company, location, and vertical segments to generate leads. I used research to ferret out the people who used to work with the executives I was targeting and would then talk to them before I made that first call to the candidate.

So, with time, I became very good at getting through to executives and starting the initial conversation. My exploits went mainstream when CBC television followed me around on an actual search project back in the mid 1990s. But I needed to find a way to convert that first great call into a meeting with my client: A promising call often went nowhere when the executive candidate had to stop and prepare a résumé for my client. Truth be known, if you're not looking for a job, and not sold on the opportunity 100 percent, it takes a lot of energy to sit down and craft a résumé. Because they weren't looking, they always had to do it from scratch, which is even worse. People hate writing résumés. In fact I was once told by a CEO that he would rather have his wisdom teeth pulled than write a résumé.

The job of résumé writing often fell on me, and I too hated it. Fortunately, years ago I met Mark Haluska. It was when I partnered with him on our first joint search that I discovered a tool he had invented called the Confidential Candidate Brief (CCB), which let him allow executive prospects to screen themselves in, did all the grunt work for him, and gave a more accurate picture of the individual's qualifications relative to the job to be filled.

I quickly learned that Mark had been having the same issue with star performers having neither the time nor interest in writing a résumé, which I'm not afraid to admit is the single biggest obstacle I've encountered recruiting executives and bringing them forward in a timely manner. Mark solved this problem himself and shared it with me. I adopted it, with his blessing, instantly.

The battlefield strategist Liddell Hart summed it up years ago, when he coined the term "the indirect approach." It means you don't keep banging head-first into the problem—that just makes it worse.

Attacking the trenches head-on in World War I was a tragic example. Instead, do something surprising—something that maneuvers around the blockage. In World War II, the Germans attacked through the supposedly impassible Ardennes forest, sweeping around the flanks of the French army's famed Maginot Line and surprising them from their rear. This was a classic indirect approach. In our case, the blockage is always the executives' need to write a résumé to pursue an opportunity in which they're not sure they're even interested. Previous to your calling they were perfectly happy and content working at their present company. That's the inertia you have to overcome.

Mark's CCB answered the question of how to apply the indirect approach to recruiting. Essentially, what the CCB does is help screen the "I haven't got the time to write a résumé this week" executives into the search almost effortlessly. Instead of letting the résumé issue hold him back, Mark created a form he sent to the people he was most interested in, allowing them to answer a few questions and mail or e-mail it back to him. The CCB is comprised of a dozen or so questions that hit on the hot buttons or issues most critical to the employer's search requirement.

The CCB is introduced to the candidate at the end of our first phone call. Qualified and interested prospects are offered the opportunity to complete a CCB. The CCB is presented as a tool to replace the executive prospect's need to create a résumé. Answering the questions takes no more than a half hour for most executives to complete. The end result for us and our clients is a detailed account of the potential candidate's skills and experience as they relate to the exact position we're looking to fill. Our clients have become spoiled by the CCB, and don't want to see a candidate presented without an accompanying CCB.

The benefits are many:

- Explicitly focused on the needs of you, the employer, as detailed in your job description and marketed to the candidate's WIFM, as gleaned from their position profile.

- Unobtrusive.

- Fast turnaround.

- It acts as the candidate's first interview.

The lessons from this indirect approach are simple to state (albeit somewhat difficult to think up in the first place!):

- Understand your market, so you emphasize the strengths of your client company. An indirect approach that's badly focused will backfire.

- Know what would appeal in that market to the best candidates—what will drive them to admire your client?

- Above all: Sincerity wins. These days, people are dying for a hint of meaning in their lives. Connect your indirect campaign to your candidate's WIFM and you're golden.

Confidential Candidate Brief for Tulip COO search.

The Confidential Candidate Brief (CCB) is not something we borrowed from another search firm. It's unique to our search practices. You can, however, create your own with the example in Appendix B and by cross-referencing the questions to both statements made in the position profile and requirements detailed in the job description. If you want to turn every passive candidate into a live prospect, use an indirect approach to position the company as we do with the confidential candidate brief. Ultimately, it's much easier to get the top people to call you than for you to chase them.

Surprisingly, Mark and I both have had candidates initially rejected by a company when they were submitted via a résumé alone. Many of those same candidates were then resubmitted, but this time the résumé was accompanied by the candidate's CCB. These same companies then decided that they *did* want to see the candidate, and many of those people were ultimately hired! This proves a résumé alone isn't enough, because that perfect candidate just might slip through your fingers.

YOUR INTERVIEW GUIDE

After writing your job description, position profile, and confidential candidate brief, draft a detailed interview guide to take you through the next steps. The guide will contain behavioral interview questions linked to the competencies required in the role. Many questions will be unique to the role, and each successive step in the process will also prompt new questions. It's neither possible nor advisable to ask all the questions in one session since it would make the interview more like an interrogation. There will be adequate time to address all the questions needed to select the correct person. By the time the successful candidate has been selected, that candidate will have met with everyone involved. He or she will have invested more than a dozen hours answering and asking questions to be certain their accepting the role will be mutually beneficial for themselves and the company. You should consult with HR about what questions *not* to ask and areas *not* to venture into in a candidate's past, but only *after* completing your draft interview guide.

> James McNerney, Jr., the outgoing CEO and current chairman of Boeing, publicly stated he was not interested in the job at Boeing when he was originally approached. In fact, he had previously stated that he wanted to stay at 3M. After accepting the new role at Boeing, McNerney said that he wanted to "close out his career at a higher-profile company that presents a bigger management challenge."[3] I suspect Mr. McNerney's decision to reconsider Boeing's challenge was one that took a good deal of time and input.

Note of caution: Make no mistake as to the candidate's mindset. Assuming your ESP has performed a deep dive search to uncover the best candidate for the job and not just the most available candidate, it is very likely *you'll* need the candidate more than the candidate needs you. Therefore, tread carefully. For some reason, after spending an enormous amount of time ensuring that only the cream of the crop is presented at the interview stage, I've seen many unskilled interviewers—from human resources to the ultimate hiring authority—look for reasons to disqualify a candidate. Such caution is understandable, to an extent, but it must be controlled since the candidate may sense and reciprocate the sentiment and start looking for reasons to disqualify *you*.

They don't need you, your company, or your opportunity. They likely already have everything they need. They're there because they are curious about the opportunity presented to them in an enticing manner by the ESP (which we discuss in the next chapter). So the due diligence interviews must be conducted professionally, and these highly sought-after executives should be treated with the appropriate decorum. The candidates will form impressions about your company with each interaction—from security desk to executive boardroom— and one misstep along the way could sour the candidate on the opportunity.

With the exception of HR, many senior executives are not fully conscious of what *may or may not* be asked in an interview. This is a serious matter. In this day and age of political correctness and extremism, it would be a sound idea to run your questions by a senior member of your HR staff to ensure compliance with current laws.

Bear in mind, you're not asking for HR's permission to ask what is needed, but rather if the questions are legal. "The legality of interview questions and HR involvement aside, do not be tempted to have HR actually fashion your interview questions. If you do, you are likely to receive a series of questions that very closely follow a prepared job description. Rarely if ever do questions based on a job description allow for one to weigh the essential skills, behaviors, and cultural fit necessary for success," says Janette Levey-Frisch, Esq.

Could your "tried and true" hiring practices expose you to employment litigation?

As further preparation we suggest downloading a short guide provided to our readers by Janette Levey-Frisch, Esq., titled *Could Your "Tried and True" Hiring Practices Expose You to Employment Litigation?*

The sequence of documents runs as follows: from left to right, starting with the business plan to the onboarding plan. Please see the diagram shown in Figure 3.4.

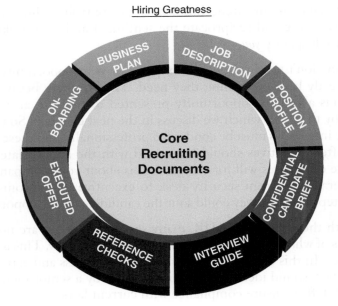

Figure 3.4   Core executive recruiting documents.

NOTES

1. www.gallup.com/poll/181289/majority-employees-not-engaged-despite-gains-2014.aspx.
2. http://sethgodin.typepad.com/seths_blog/2008/01/permission-mark.html.
3. Alexei Barrionuevo, "Boeing Pay Is a Match for Chief," *New York Times*, July 7, 2005.

CHAPTER 4

Positioning the Opportunity

The Quick and the Dead

Research is to see what everybody else has seen, and to think what nobody else has thought.

—Albert Szent-Gyorgyi

Meanwhile, back at the ranch, Michael and I discussed our outreach strategy. We quickly defined our target market, our message, and the marketing and recruiting materials we needed. Time was of the essence because the role had been open for an extended period.

Because of Michael's strong manufacturing background and superior understanding of the role's technical aspects, he took an indirect approach. An indirect strategy normally involves advertising and asking for referrals—Michael believed he understood the role and that he had sufficient contacts in the industry to pull it off. I, meanwhile, chose the direct approach. This involves deep research into the major players in an industry ecosystem. Off we went, still a team but more like Ferrari or McLaren than the LA Dodgers or New York Yankees—our competitive fires were blazing, and each of us personally wanted to win the race.

Michael took off out of the blocks, quickly placing an ad on LinkedIn. This was Michael's first major executive search under my tutelage. I had explained to Michael when he joined the firm that although posting a job might seem the easiest and quickest way to generate a plethora of candidates, it's often a complete waste of time. But he was intent on trying it his way, and I let him proceed. Some repeatedly cast nets and others use lasers. Because of my previous experience as a researcher, I opted for the road less traveled with some new (at the time) tools in my arsenal like ZoomInfo and ExecuNet.

Michael was initially elated—borderline smug, actually—after receiving numerous responses from LinkedIn. But after vetting the responses more carefully he realized most of them were shot in the dark-type replies that didn't seem to fit the role in spite of his very detailed job specifications. On the other hand, using ZoomInfo I sourced a list of nearly every chief operating officer, vice-president of manufacturing, and vice-president of operations—as well as related titles—in the Milwaukee area. And even though I was faced with the unenviable task of calling and qualifying every single one of them, this was a good problem to have in my mind. Before ZoomInfo and the like facilitated such easy data search capabilities, it would have taken several professional researchers two or three weeks to build a similar list.

At this point, Michael was buried under paper. His indirect ad campaign produced more than 700 résumés and at least as many phone calls, messages, and e-mails. He had to respond to at least some of them, of course, and it took him five weeks—full time—to narrow them down. And to be honest, he got what most other recruiters would get by using the same approach: underqualified, uninteresting responses. His experience is why I use a laser instead of a fishing net. I've done both, and the laser is unquestionably more effective. And you don't spend time defending your standards or criteria to a multitude of responders whom you know don't qualify anyhow.

Instead, I seek out a select core of desired candidates and target all my expertise and effort on them. I'm looking for a perfect fit. That's what we get paid for. It's why we dive deep into each corporate abyss, often pushing exploration beyond the traditional frontiers to elevate board awareness and commitment to fully identify their company's future needs.

Lap two. As our friendly competition heated up, the optics were that I was behind. I then played the two aces I already mentioned—ZoomInfo and ExecuNet. I posted a scrupulously detailed description of the job requirement on ExecuNet, inviting interested candidates to go to our website for more information. What distinguishes ExecuNet from other networking sites like LinkedIn is that it's a closed, private network. You must meet a threshold of experience and tenure to be allowed inside. And once in, most members stick around after finding a job because of the camaraderie and the fact that it's a good place to recruit their own teams. I've used ExecuNet since the late 1980s, and

CEO Dave Opton wrote the foreword for my second best-selling book, *Guerrilla Marketing for Job Hunters.*

I then turned to ZoomInfo.com to compile a list of the chairpersons of the boards of some of the largest manufacturing companies in Milwaukee. After paring the list of initial contacts down to 10 qualified candidates, I appealed directly to the chairs of all 10 organizations via a courier package containing a personal note attached to the position profile. I followed up with a voicemail regarding the search and what I was looking for from them.

This approach was similar to the "networking with the newly departed" tactic I teach job hunters in my book *Guerilla Marketing for Job Hunters 3.0.* Speaking with former employees can be the quickest way to get a behind-the-scenes profile on a company to assess what value you might bring to them and whether or not they're worth pursuing. You can then use that information after forming a clear picture, from several sources, to help shape your conversation with the prospect.

It's critical to be knowledgeable about the inner workings of your target industry because prospects will only deal with people they regard as peers. If you can't speak their language, the call will be short and probably unproductive.

Calling the chair of the board of 10 of the largest manufacturers had an unexpected result, however. Originally, I was intent on simply asking for recommendations on whom to speak to get an overview of Milwaukee's operations leaders. The unexpected result was that eight of the 10 chairpersons returned my calls. Six of them told me my ideal candidate actually did exist, *but*—and it was a major *but*—the fellow had retired.

I spent between 10 and 20 minutes with each of the chairs, and half of each call was focused on why this one particular person was so good. It's unusual for more than one person to recommend the same person, let alone six people. So I was more than curious. Each chair, in his or her own way, extolled Jim's virtues and indicated he'd have the best knowledge on who's available right now—not a primary consideration—and, more importantly to me at least, who's exceptional.

It was during one of these calls that I discovered that Jim was only 55 years old. He'd served his entire career with the same company and had risen through the ranks from the shop floor to EVP Operations over a 30-year span. The fact that he'd served that long and gone that far made me very interested in him as a candidate, and not just as a source of information or referrals.

Coaxing someone out of retirement, however, is tricky and usually a waste of time. It takes an extraordinary person to reverse the inertia of retirement and its accompanying mental hiatus. It often ends in disaster. Occasionally, though, you do meet a Type A who's having a hard time adjusting to a slower pace and still has enough juice for a 5- to 10-year run. Let's just say their "honey-do" list of chores around the cottage is all caught up, and they're antsy to get back in the game.

So, as always, I did my research before calling him. My opening line was, "Jim, this is David Perry, and I've got to ask you: Are you tired of painting the house yet?"

There was a long pause.

Then, in a slightly irritated voice reminiscent of John Wayne's *True Grit* drawl: "Who is this? What do you want?"

"My name is David Perry. Last week 6 out of 10 chairmen of the boards I contacted in Milwaukee regarding an executive search for a COO told me you were perfect. And then they all kinda laughed at me saying I was too late, you had retired. So let me ask you again, Jim—how's your 'honey-do' list coming along?"

In less than 15 seconds I had his attention, but I knew I was likely annoying him more than anything. Sometimes, though, you need to strike to the core to get someone like Jim's attention. An executive with his profile would have fielded hundreds of calls from recruiters over the years. I had only one chance to start a conversation. I could feel Jim lean in to the mouthpieces.

"Describe the job for me," he demanded in a low, gravelly voice. I brushed his question aside. I knew this was where most calls stalled and deals died. I don't give good phone. I'm not slick. I discovered a long time ago I lack the verbal acuity of most of the former successful recruiters I'd met, so I compensate with brutal honesty.

"I'm a lousy salesman, Jim," I said. "I couldn't possibly explain this opportunity over the phone well enough to hold your interest for more than a few seconds. Instead, Jim, the position profile has all the details clearly written out and I'd like to send it to you if you want to see it. When you have five minutes of quiet time you can sit down and read the profile, and I think you'll agree with those who recommended you for the position. You're perfect for the role. Then we can discuss your requirements. Does that work for you?"

I knew it was a gamble. Retirement may have been right up Jim's alley, for all I knew. The man could have fielded 10 calls from other recruiters this week alone and might have been on the verge of hanging up on me, leaving me practically at square one.

But sometimes, gambles pay off.

It's Go Time!

Much like my experience recruiting for Tulip, we're nearing the halfway point of your transformation into a savvy acquirer of talent. So let's recap your incredible progress:

- You've nailed down a succinct and engaging job description and all search committee members are on board.

- You've created an enticing position profile that speaks to the role's broad scope and unbridled potential.

- You've crafted an impressive CCB that will intrigue candidates and compel them to engage your sophisticated and confidential executive search process.

Now it's time to start recruiting, right? No. Not yet. Not if you want to find and hire the most desirable executives.

Let me explain: Hiring greatness is all about adequate planning. Alan Lakein phrased it well when he quipped that, "Planning is bringing the future into the present so that you can do something about it now."

But then again, some people erroneously assume they've planned adequately and haven't—and it's impossible to tell them otherwise, no matter how much dung they get into. It reminds me of the story of the frequent grizzly bear attacks occurring near a tourist hiking area of a rugged northern British Columbia town. Legend has it that, no matter how clearly wildlife officials warned hikers to stay well away, inevitably another hiker would ignore the warnings and attempt to feed or photograph them. Most thought they were adequately prepared since they were carrying bells or pepper spray. At a loss as to how to convince people to avoid getting killed by grizzly bears, the authorities finally erected the sign shown in Figure 4.1.

> ### B.C. Fish and Wildlife Branch
>
> ### WARNING: GRIZZLY BEAR ATTACKS
>
> 1. Due to the frequency of human–bear encounters, the B.C. Fish and Wildlife Branch is advising hikers, hunters, fishermen, and any persons who use the outdoors in a recreational or work-related function to take extra precautions while in the field.
>
> 2. Some outdoorsmen wear little noisy bells on clothing so as to give advance warning to any bears that might be close by so they don't take them by surprise.
>
> 3. Some outdoorsmen carry pepper spray with them in case of an encounter with a bear.
>
> 4. All outdoorsmen should also be on the watch for fresh bear activity, and be able to tell the difference between black bear feces and grizzly bear feces. Black bear feces is smaller and contains lots of berries and squirrel fur. Grizzly bear shit has bells in it and smells like pepper.

Figure 4.1   Grizzly bear attacks.

Finding top executives is a bit like hiking with grizzlies in the mountains. You need to plan effectively or you—and your company—could end up smelling like pepper. Better to heed Lakein's advice and bring your future corporate vision into the present by aligning with passionate executive leadership that can "do something about the future now." You need a strategic road map.

Before recruiting Tulip's chief operations officer, Michael and I created a candidate road map as a guide. First we decided where to look for the best candidates and, specifically, with whom to talk. Most fail to fully understand the extensive research undertaken by professional executive search firms, but such research is pivotal to success.

SEARCH RESEARCH: THE BLACK BOX

In commercial enterprises, both the vice-presidents of sales and marketing invest a lot of time and money precisely targeting prospects. Companies spend billions of dollars each year on research, focus groups, and consumer studies because it provides useful strategic feedback. Successful companies are relentless in their quest to precisely define and target their market to sell more while spending less time, money, and effort. They know that prequalified buyers are more likely to buy.

Similarly, buried deep in the inner sanctum of most retained search firms is a cadre of recruiting sherpas. These are often quiet and soft-spoken professionals who use their skills and tools to provide search consultants with competitive intelligence, constructing org charts by filtering through an elaborate maze of corporate titles and reporting structures to reveal executives who have the exact skills and specific experience your open job requires. The researcher's expertise is in finding the proverbial "needle in a haystack of needles—your needle."

As your vice-president of sales knows, it's easy for field reps to burn through cash talking to suspects instead of having intelligent conversations, which turn prospects into buyers. It's the same for recruiters. With thoughtful research they can qualify whom they talk to about your company's vacant position. Research takes time up-front, but will save countless hours speaking with unqualified people with the added plus of keeping your hiring plans confidential. You exponentially increase the likelihood of attracting the right executive to your team when you do proper search research.

The rigor associated with such thorough research is incredibly time-consuming. While we don't expect you to do your own research, it's important to understand the process so you'll know what your ESP is doing on your behalf. Set the bar high and challenge your ESP. Insist your ESP demonstrate his or her advanced research capabilities. And hold your ESP accountable for results.

The Difference between a Recruitment Approach and a Search Approach

Poor or nonexistent research is responsible for most failed executive search projects. It's where most search consultants stumble out of the gate, and thanks to that we've had a lot of experience parachuting in to salvage a floundering search assignment. In each such case, the common denominator has been the poor quality of research done in advance. It's important to understand why this happens so you can avoid making the same mistake.

In the old days—10 years ago—the recruiting industry suddenly split into two well-defined groups. Original research was the key differentiator between the two camps. Retained executive search firms, like every other management consulting business, operated on behalf of the client and were paid a retainer, hence their providing meaningful research was paramount. Service was the name of the game. Candidate quality, not quantity of deals closed, was the measurement metric of the day for these firms.

Contingency firms, on the other hand, are paid only if one of their candidates is hired. Because there's no upfront cost associated with hiring a contingency search firm, around a decade ago it became fashionable in HR circles to have dozens of firms simultaneously working the same assignment. When this happens, recruiters are under enormous pressure to close clients quickly—otherwise they end up working for free. Speed and assignment turnover are critical to winning in that game.

The two types of firms both use the "executive search" moniker but contingency firms often do no research, relying instead on advertising or their own database of potential candidates. Because of this and much to the dismay of HR, often companies using more than one contingency firm on an assignment are forced to suffer through a wave of duplicate résumés. That's because contingency recruiters tend to all fish from the same pond.

That said, the distinction between retained and contingency firms has blurred somewhat over the last decade. Online tools like LinkedIn, along with the proliferation of job boards for finding and recruiting actively looking people, have put downward pressure on search firm fees. To compete, many firms don't undertake any original research.

But while technology has certainly made it easier to identify executives, recruiting them has become more challenging. The best executives are zealously guarded from the outside world by an army of assistants—and technology—who are specifically instructed to thwart ESPs and their ilk. For some, the effort needed to cull the type of intelligence afforded by traditional search research is harder than ever. The benefits, I assure you, are worth the extra effort.

Today it's not uncommon for a recruiter to skip the research stage when trying to earn a fee. Over the past 10 years many ESPs—who survived the last several recessions—have succumbed to performing a quick file search, phoning around to a couple of companies in obvious turmoil, then running an ad and surfing LinkedIn with hopes of attracting your future star executive. The results are predictably poor, and not what you need to consistently win the war for talent.

The research phase of a search is another key difference between a recruiting approach and a search approach. A recruitment company will put together a list of people they already know and who are in their database, or who came through a referral channel. A search firm, alternatively, conducts new research for each and every assignment.

When to Fire Your Recruiter

If, after a few weeks on your project, your ESP brings you a list with the names and titles of your competitors' top people—*fire them!*

That's not research. That's just a list of names. Unfortunately as lines between retained and contingency firms continue to blur, the recruiting industry and HR have begun using the terms "executive search research" and "name generation" interchangeably. We've seen the output of both and the list of names is just that: a list of names designed to impress you. Name generation is not synonymous with search research. The class of business intelligence you need to effectively hire greatness will only be provided by full-fledged researchers.

Sadly, most candidate lists offer less insight than the white pages directory you abandoned years ago for Google. The most valuable information goes deeper than name and title. Search research is the by-product of continuous and diligent investigation of individuals and situations, and is business intelligence that provides context and depth. Online databases are plentiful and easy to access, but names alone aren't the prize—intelligence is. Search research is akin to a functional SWOT analysis of the good, the bad, and the ugly details of your competitor's executives.

Search researchers start by looking to understand:

- Which companies are winning, and why? (Industry, geography, economic climate)

- Who are the leaders driving the bus? (Who holds the reins— name, title, span of authority, direct reports, Capex and Opex budgets—the full org chart)

You need to determine the winners and losers, as well as the context and business climate. A client once assured me, "Even turkeys can fly with a good back wind." Search research will examine the circumstances and context, not just the end result.

Texas Hold'em versus Fantasy Football

Is your recruiting philosophy holding you back? Many companies, such as AMESS Software (mentioned earlier in the book), gambled with their executive recruiting process. These companies aim too low and settle for what's offered, instead of setting their sights on the best. AMESS Software was like that. Their CEO's meager aspirations were rarely disappointed by great talent. The CEO tried to play Texas Hold'em by hiring slow and firing fast and frequently. He soon cycled through the entire deck of sales vice-presidents in his town, and had no better luck recruiting elsewhere.

Instead of playing Texas Hold'em and accepting the talent you're dealt, I invite you to think differently. Change the rules. Stack the deck. Draw an inside straight—every time.

Tell me honestly, how well could your company perform if you could consistently recruit your industry's top people? What if you always had the inside track to recruiting the best executive talent: Would you chose to build a different team? If you could always recruit whom you wanted, would you accomplish your goals quicker? What if we told you how to flip that Texas Hold'em deck of cards to see the face value of each card in the deck, legally and without getting shot? I suppose you could draw a royal flush with every hand. You could win all the time.

Actually, forget the card analogy. There are only 52 of them, after all. We're going to show you how to play even bigger and assure your company's destiny.

Supersize Your Thinking

Successful search research really has more in common with Fantasy Football than Texas Hold'em. Instead of limiting yourself to a deck of 52 meager cards, Fantasy Football provides an abundance of highly talented players to choose from. There are 32 NFL teams, as well as hundreds of college teams to recruit from: the best in the world and the up-and-comers! You can quickly find player-specific statistics on every quarterback, running back, wide receiver, tight end, kicker, left tackle you name it. Every player's performance information is available for analysis. Whether it's offense or defense or bench strength you're looking for, you can see it all online: completions, attempts, yards, touchdowns, and interceptions. Statistics on football players are available on dozens of Internet websites.

While many consider Fantasy Football just a game, supporters spend real money as well as their own time hunting painstakingly for an edge gathering their own intelligence on players in addition to information freely available to everyone. In the same vein, search research can help you create detailed performance profiles on every executive you'd possibly consider—before you even meet him or her. This additional layer of business intelligence facilitates comparing the performance of an identified group against another, as well as against a host of variables including company size, geography, market positioning, brand maturity, and even company culture.

A robust search research function can create an environment in which you can continuously recruit high performance teams by design. How valuable is that?

Search Research: Reimagined

Exceptional researchers adopt an abundance mindset. Think Fantasy Football, not Texas Hold'em. They consider every executive as available, all the time. They don't limit themselves, except for any hands-off restrictions, to examining only executives already in their database. Just recruiting the low-hanging fruit limits your company's growth potential. Instead, identify which executives are the best. Set your sights on them. Then go get them!

The case study we've kept coming back to in this book— that of Fred's chief operating officer/successor search—is a good example. In the book's first chapter, when I first met Fred, I asked him questions regarding the hands-off client restrictions (Figure 4.2) of the first two search firms. His responses led me to immediately take the assignment. We realized that the search had not been executed correctly, with the failed consultants being tripped up by their firms' hands-off obligations.

> ### Side Note:
>
> The client hands-off restriction policy, which is upheld by all reputable search firms, has forced many experienced ESPs to leave major firms and establish their own boutique firms where they are able to service their clients properly without onerous hands-off restrictions.

Figure 4.2   Hands-Off Restrictions.

Just like Fred, you deserve to select from the best of the best. Yes, leaders are rare. Yes, executive talent is scarce. But when you approach the recruiting process with an assumption of abundance—that all talent is available all the time—you won't limit yourself to the traditional pool of talent in your industry.

How to Do Search Research Correctly

In our case, Michael and I looked at all the companies, organizations, and businesses in Tulip's ecosystem, including suppliers and customers. We talked to executives within the local manufacturing association as well.

Geographically, we specifically targeted direct and indirect competitors within a 90-minute drive of the manufacturing plant in Milwaukee. Wherever practical, start a search physically close to where the executive will work and expand outward in concentric circles (like a bull's-eye target in archery). While this isn't always possible, a tightly targeted search focused around local geography can reduce the time and expense associated with relocating an executive.

Preparing for a Deep Dive

Whether you do the research yourself or farm it out, you'll need to dive into the details and examine the minutiae to create meaningful intelligence. So where to begin? You could hire a search firm to do it since research is a first step for them, but I encourage you to do some research yourself first. If you begin the research in advance of hiring the search consultant, you'll understand where the search firm should focus its efforts along with having a good idea on what intelligence gathering you really need from them. You'll also know if your ESP is doing everything possible for your project.

The quickest way to build a preliminary list is to gather your Search Committee, and have your head of human resources lead you through a facilitated exercise to determine:

- What companies are the best sources of executive talent that suit your needs?

- Where does this talent profile reside now?

  - Industries
  - Competitors

    - Direct
    - Indirect

  - Suppliers
  - Vendors

- What functional position[s] do they hold?

- What specific titles are associated with this role?

- What trends or events might magnetize them to your company?

- What issues may push them away from their current company or industry? (Typical examples include takeovers and mergers, and industry consolidations.)

In our Texas Hold'em versus Fantasy Football analogy, it's the difference between choosing among 52 known entities and hundreds, perhaps thousands of the best executives in the world. Your initial list may be huge, but a researcher with an abundance mentality can easily winnow down an impressive yet unwieldy list to a manageable number of all-stars.

Figure 4.3   **Candidate universe ecosystem.**

Once you have your preliminary target list, here's how to further calibrate your thinking to quickly hone in on the best qualified executives to approach. Search research permits you to ask, and answer, the following (see Figure 4.3):

- Who are your competitors' top executives?

- Which executives have already demonstrated they can do what your position requires?

  - Which among them can figuratively blow the doors off the place?

- What can you find out about him or her?

  - Responsibilities

  - Accomplishments

- Strengths/weaknesses
- Track record
- Career aspirations

- Why might they be interested in your opportunity?

To do this correctly, you must understand their span of authority and that of the team they manage. That's the only way to relate them to your needs. After building the list of ideal executives to recruit, you need to ask a new set of questions:

- Who knows them, has worked for them, and can tell you how they might fit in your organization? Can they offer you insight? An introduction maybe?

- How do I get in front of them? What's the best way to connect?

- What message do I need to deliver to get their attention and start a dialogue?

Where do you turn to start collecting this information? There are online databases aplenty, but we also use other tools to help cut weeks off the research process and do deep dives to collect information normally unavailable to a recruiter.

The best tool we've ever used to identify senior executives, managers, and high-end individual contributors, and has been a staple in our tool kit since the turn of this century, is ZoomInfo (see Figure 4.4). The site has been a pioneer and perennial leader in the B2B marketing data business since it was founded by CEO Jonathan Stern in 2000 as Eliyon Technologies. We serendipitously became a beta tester for ZoomInfo in its formative years.

It is more important to reach the people who count than to count the people you reach.

—**Anonymous**

Figure 4.4   ZoomInfo profile.

ZoomInfo's power, breadth of information, and simplicity of use cannot be overstated. But it's not just the raw processing power. Zoom-Info's technology uses *automatic summarization* to reduce information from hundreds of thousands of news and information sources to create summaries, which retain the most important points of the original document.[1]

In our practice, we use ZoomInfo to search, sort, monitor, and continuously update key information that's pertinent to each of our projects. It's more refined than Google Alerts and faster. In less than a second, you can retrieve the same type of detailed research that used to take a researcher two to three weeks to compile. You can stay current on 136 million people and 8.5 million companies. There are also handy features that allow you to set alerts, gather more intelligence from social media sites like Facebook and LinkedIn, as well as numerous ways to share profiles between coworkers.

Groundbreaking Changes in Technology Make It Easier to Find People ...

... But More Difficult to Reach Executives

Technology has been the great equalizer for the executive search industry, allowing boutique firms to compete with giants without the need to be heavily staffed with researchers. Prior to the proliferation of online databases and social networking sites, a search firm's Rolodex was its currency. An ESP's major value was his or her quick access to the résumés, profiles, and business contacts their firm had amassed for decades. And then suddenly technology put millions of people at the fingertips of recruiters, human resource departments, and hiring managers. Unfortunately, being able to find more people faster *did not* equate to attracting more talent, and if you've ever watched the NBC television show *America's Got Talent* you know exactly what I'm talking about.

The introduction of job boards like Monster and social networking sites like LinkedIn in the late 1990s and early 2000s made it relatively easy for job hunters to find open positions and employers to find people. This initially diminished the value of a recruiter's résumé database. But then, a funny thing happened: It became too easy for job hunters to apply for jobs. Chaos ensued, along with a rapid transformation in hiring practices that went unnoticed by both those looking for work and employers.

Allow me to explain.

For each of the past five years, 50-plus million jobs have been filled in the United States—almost *all without a job posting*— because of the proliferation of job boards and social media sites like LinkedIn. While creating job postings can keep an HR staff ultra-busy in countless organizations, many other employers are reticent to post jobs because they can't deal with the avalanche of résumés they get—much less deal with the subsequent (increased) government regulations for maintaining records on those job applicants. Today, savvy employers rely on a brand-new *digital* suite of tools and tactics to find the handful of most qualified recruits to interview.

The recruiting paradigm has shifted, and this revolution in recruiting has taken place at the same time the job market feels itself under huge strain. The current state of the global job market is more challenging than it has been in more than 25 years. The magnitude of job force reductions has been unprecedented. When you think about the quantity of people vying for the few known job openings that might exist, employers need to be clever and think outside the box to separate the wheat from the chaff.

At the same time, executives have become loath to being treated like online commodities. They've also become increasingly distrustful of unsolicited calls from recruiters. For this reason alone, many senior executives now covet a low profile and purposefully avoid social media whenever and wherever possible. Social networking profiles are only as reliable as the user who has entered the information, and that information can be biased toward a specific end result—like being recruited. (*Guerrilla Marketing for Job Hunters 3.0* goes into great depth on how to leverage LinkedIn for that purpose.)

Social networking sites frequently lack details around span of authority and rarely provide detailed org charts. In many cases the information is also out of date. This means there are large holes in the intelligence required to recruit that individual. A recent study showed that "a full 68 percent of Fortune 500 CEOs still have no presence on social media. However, that finding is an improvement by two percentage points over last year's results."[2] Anecdotal evidence from more than 500 executive search projects over the past 10 years supports these findings.

There's also still a sizable chunk of people who don't use social media due to concerns about privacy, data security, potential identity theft, and/or because they don't want to appear as though they're looking for a job.

Be Vigilant

Titles and responsibilities are rarely equivalent across companies or industries. The secret is to isolate the desired skills and experience from the designated responsibilities. When creating your candidate pipeline you need to amass the org charts of all executives among your company's competitors, regardless of title or current functional role, who have the experience and skills matching your requirements. You should also include executives who currently reside within other areas of your company's ecosystem. For example, many years ago, when assigned to recruit an executive vice-president of logistics for a multibillion-dollar telecommunications firm, we identified and recruited a vice-president of operations from a PC manufacturer because he was formerly the Navy flag officer responsible for a $20-billion supply chain.

Better questions bring better insight. The more effort you put into the front end of an executive search, especially when it comes to calibrating research, the less time you'll spend kissing frogs because each meeting/interview will be on point and your time well spent. This

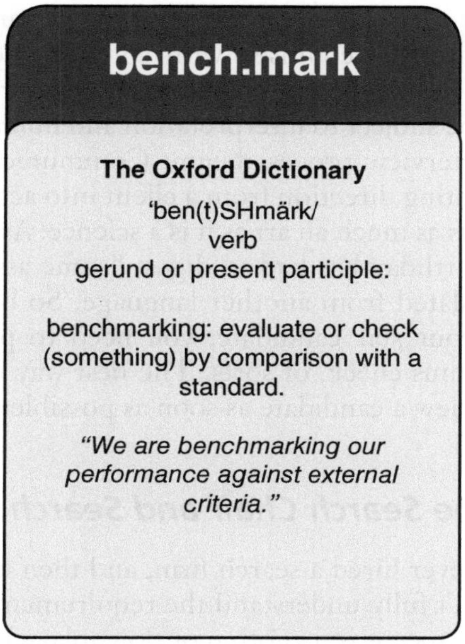

bench.mark

The Oxford Dictionary

'ben(t)SHmärk/
verb
gerund or present participle:

benchmarking: evaluate or check
(something) by comparison with a
standard.

*"We are benchmarking our
performance against external
criteria."*

Figure 4.5   Bench mark picture.

greatly enhances the experience and will make closing on your ideal candidate easier, but a side benefit is the stealth nature of this approach. In today's hypercompetitive market, the less your competitors know about your operation and future plans the better, and when your outreach campaign is this highly focused you alert fewer people to your plans.

As your research is being completed, you can clarify more precisely what your prospective candidates should look like by benchmarking (see Figure 4.5) from a known executive who's deemed a fit.

BENCHMARKING

Matching a candidate's skills and experience with a company's requirements is usually fairly straightforward, mostly because technical greatness in a specific function like marketing, sales, or finance is situational. Used correctly, a confidential candidate brief becomes a literal checklist of primary information. The real challenge in every executive search is to ensure alignment between the company's values and those of the candidate, which is often referred to as "fit."

But as every parent knows, hearing isn't the same as listening—which also shouldn't be confused with comprehending. No matter how much time and effort goes into defining your ideal candidate, you'll inevitably be subject to interpretation and human error once the recruiting and interview process begin. Communication is always a challenge. Translating direction from a client into actionable, competitive intelligence is as much an art as it is a science: Ask any parent who on their child's birthday has had to digest "some assembly required" instructions translated from another language. So before diving into the market for your star candidate, you need to perform a critical final check—a litmus check, of sorts. The best way to ensure fit is to benchmark interview a candidate as soon as possible.

Calibrating the Search Chair and Search Consultant

Anyone who has ever hired a search firm, and then months later realized the firm didn't fully understand the requirements or that a major component of the spec was forgotten or downplayed, understands just how easy it is to waste time looking for the wrong person. But this simply doesn't happen if you benchmark at the front end. Granted, it adds slightly more up-front work for the search consultant and Search Chair. But it can also reduce the amount of time spent finding the perfect individual by 50 percent or more. When you know exactly what you're looking for from the fit side, the never-going-to-work-out candidates become obvious. Lost opportunity costs may never be recovered, so dropping a lit match on the haystack to quickly reveal the golden needle within is never a bad idea.

In executive search, benchmarking is the practice of choosing a candidate to interview to gauge both the search consultant and the Search Chair's alignment on the skills, experience, and fit needed for that role. Every time you do a search, you need to benchmark.

Think of it as a dry run to calibrate both sides and validate the requirements before the search consultant goes to the marketplace. This an opportunity to tighten/alter the position profile and confidential candidate brief, as well as potentially the thinking of the Search Committee (and its chair) to ensure everyone's on the same page. It's also an opportunity for the search consultant to understand how the Search Chair processes information and draws conclusions, which is a good time for the search consultant to offer support if there are any obvious gaps in the Search Chair's interview and assessment knowledge.

Heidrick & Struggles is one of the largest search firms in the world, and its CEO Kevin Kelly revealed in a *Financial Times* article that a recent internal study of 20,000 Heidrick searches found that "40 percent of executives hired at the senior level are pushed out, fail, or quit within 18 months. It's expensive in terms of lost revenue. It's expensive in terms of the individual's hiring. It's damaging to morale . . . ."

Because of the above it's imperative for companies to adopt a comprehensive approach to executive hiring and retention practices. The odds are good that these companies will be engaged in an executive search in the near future, and the likelihood of failure is astronomical: Recent studies by the Corporate Executive Board show that "50 to 70 percent of executives fail within the first 18 months of promotion into an executive role, either from within or coming from outside the organization; of those, about 3 percent 'fail spectacularly,' while nearly 50 percent 'quietly struggle.'"[4]

Lack of preparation for C-level roles is a significant factor in this shocking failure rate. An extensive, 10-year study of executive performance by Navalent, a leadership consulting firm, concluded—after over 2,600 Fortune 1000 executive interviews—that:

- 76 percent of respondents indicated the formal development processes of their organization were not, or at best minimally, helpful in preparing them for their executive role.

- 55 percent indicated that they had minimal, if any, ongoing coaching and feedback to help them refine their ability to perform in an executive role.

- 45 percent indicated they had minimal understanding of the challenges they would face in an executive role.[5]

Today's young executives are assuming senior and C-Suite roles at an accelerated pace. Yet since they lack the experience, knowledge, relational, and emotional maturity necessary to sustain success, the failure rates we mentioned earlier are astounding but predictable. They're also consistent with this writer's extensive experience in successfully conducting over 1,000 executive search assignments over the past 30 years.

But you can avoid hiring the wrong person from the start by conducting a benchmark interview. Calibrate your needs before you take the search to market: the search becomes laser-focused when you clearly understand the complete executive profile from both a business and a fit perspective. Think about how much energy and effort goes into evaluating a candidate's technical skills, business acumen, emotional intelligence, management skills, predominant leadership style, short- and long-term goals, motivators, creativity, strengths, personality, and other factors. We're talking hours and hours of intense focused interview and assessment time, which could be better spent on viable prospects.

Who Do You Benchmark?

The benchmark candidate could be someone you both know, or an individual selected by either the search consultant or Search Chair. If it's someone from the search consultant's files, they should fit 80 percent of the technical parameters and 95 percent of the soft skills related to the fit you're looking for (not a hard and fast rule, but good to keep in mind). Considering how great of a fit they typically are, it's not unusual for the benchmark candidate to be asked back as a finalist in the search. The benchmark candidate doesn't even need to know they're the benchmark for a host of reasons, all of them in the best interest of the company. Instead recognize that the benchmark got a head start and may be in the pole position.

How to Benchmark

Approach the benchmark candidate as you would any other. After interesting them in the role, sending them the position profile (PP), as well as receiving and assessing their confidential candidate brief (CCB), simply interview the benchmark candidate in the same manner you would the others.

The opportunity for the Search Chair and search consultant (ESP) to interview and evaluate the candidate together builds a strong bond as partners in the project, each working toward a common goal.

It permits the search partners to calibrate a common understanding of what's needed to find the ideal candidate. It encourages open dialogue and discussion and can lead to refining the original job description, position profile, and CCB as required.

Following the benchmark interview a good ESP can objectively deconstruct the interview (because they lead it, with active participation from the Search Chair) to reconstruct the role and find any gaps in thinking that went into constructing the PP and/or requirements.

What To Do

The Search Chair and ESP conduct the interview together in the same room, at the same time, with the same guidelines as a regular first one-on-one interview (which is explained in-depth in section IV). The benchmark interview, however, has one major component added: following the candidate's interview, the Search Chair and ESP actively dissect the candidate's fit and experience against the PP. That discussion should assess the consultant's depth of understanding of the role from a fit standpoint, and identify where calibration is potentially needed. Experience isn't the most important item here—fit to the requirements is the goal.

And that goes beyond culture. Because you actually may *not* be looking for someone who fits in. Indeed, the position may necessitate the exact opposite. Be careful how you judge the fit against the need, as defined by the role spec'd out by the board; understand that in a turnaround, a reboot, or a whole shift of an organization, fitting in may be exactly what you don't want.

Let me explain. ...

The Benchmark Candidate in Practice

In reality, a benchmarking interview is more than just a trial run to gauge how the ESP, CCB, and Search Chair best work together. And a benchmark candidate sure isn't some stranger chosen from the firm's files at random.

When executed correctly the benchmark candidate is often the individual hired at the conclusion of a search, and is certainly a top contender for the role. So it's important to approach the interview with the same reverence you would your best customer. You want to impress them as much as they want to amaze you. Precisely because he or she is the benchmark candidate, you must treat them exactly the same as all the other candidates being interviewed. And you absolutely, positively have to ensure they're unaware others are being benchmarked against them.

By the time a client meets the benchmark candidate a number of milestones will have already occurred in rapid succession:

- The search consultant has recruited, interviewed, and screened the candidate.

- The candidate has received and reviewed the Position Profile.

- The candidate has agreed to proceed in the search and has completed the CCB, and forwarded it to the search consultant.

- The search consultant has reviewed the CCB against the position profile and often against the candidate's bio or résumé (if the candidate has a LinkedIn profile, this could be used as well).

- The search consultant has interviewed the candidate face-to-face or by phone.

The search consultant confirms through the interview process that the candidate meets the base technical qualifications and has the right experience as detailed on the CCB, and the ESP explains to the Search Chair why they consider the candidate to be fully qualified. The ESP also points out any discrepancies or weaknesses discovered ahead of time (for example, having seven years of experience if 10 years was the ideal, and why an exception is being made).

The benchmark candidate is a viable candidate at this point and will likely be asked back for further interviews, but there are certainly no guarantees. No formal referencing will have been done by this time, although informal referencing has commenced.

After the benchmark candidate's interview is over, the ESP and Search Chair discuss the candidate in detail while everything is still fresh in their minds. Both must confirm the technical skills, experience, and fit are correct. If the benchmark candidate is on target, the ESP is good to go.

If the ESP was way off in his or her assessment of fit, both ESP and Search Chair must discuss the job description, PP, and CCB in detail until it's clear where the error was made. When fit isn't assessed correctly the first time, I suggest you bring in a second benchmark candidate. Getting the fit right is critical to the long-term success of the candidate, even if it adds a week or so to the project. Accuracy must trump speed. Ensure the search parameters are correctly calibrated now, otherwise you risk wasting your time or—even worse—making a bad hire.

Communication errors happen in all lines of work. But if the fit is wrong the second time the CEO should replace the ESP, the Search Chair, or both. It's very rare that fit issues are misjudged more than once by an experienced ESP.

In the benchmark interview you'll receive feedback from the candidate about the role, which may include market intelligence that necessitates changes to the position profile. You may find you need to modify questions in the CCB to draw out overlooked aspects or more deeply assessed other areas before you meet other candidates.

The changes we usually see needing addressing are rigid educational requirements and years of experience, industry-specific competencies, and compensation. These are the issues benchmark candidates typically bring to the forefront, and that help refine your targeted pursuit. The objective is to confirm the ESP and Search Chair agree on what constitutes your ideal candidate, especially around the issue of fit. Remember: Skills and experience are really checkboxes on the candidate's CCB—fit is the wild card.

Once the ESP and Search Chair agree, it's go time!

Bottom Line

When every qualified person is considered a potential candidate, then 90 percent of the time there will be a half dozen or so excellent people to select. But there's usually one candidate who best fits the role. Many ESPs don't recognize this and only focus their strategies around the skills match. Understanding a candidate's fit is a byproduct of how you approach the recruiting and interview stage to get at the candidate's core values. To get to that point quickly you need a benchmark interview before your recruiting and interview process starts in full.

Attracting the A-Players

Many Search Committees look for executives who have been a CEO/executive of a similar-sized or larger company, and rightly so. Likewise, almost all current executives are interested in taking on a new, significant opportunity with a company of greater size to ensure they're not simply making a lateral move.

Generally, there are six reasons that motivate an executive to move to another position:

1. A final opportunity to reach the highest level of leadership within a company: They perceive they'll move from a lower potential opportunity to a higher potential opportunity.

2. They'll move from a general manager or functional role to a division president or CEO position: Higher and wider corporate visibility has taken precedence over money.

3. They'll maintain a high(er) standard of living.

4. They'll be compensated more, including a complex equation of cash, equities, net present values, and opportunity costs.

5. They envision a strong cultural fit between themselves, the board, and the company.

6. *They share the founder's passion or vision for the company.*

Along with the above, we've found the following five factors are also becoming factors for attracting executives:

1. They're doing more with less staff in their current role; they feel technologically challenged because of ever-increasing day-to-day duties previously performed by others.

2. The company is moving in a new direction.

3. Paying for higher education of college-aged children (more important than you can imagine ...).

4. Moving to a warmer climate.

5. Moving closer to aging relatives.

RECRUITING AND SCREENING

At last, you're ready to begin recruiting in earnest. Congratulations! It's been a bit of a journey, but you're finally here. Luckily, you have a long list of prospects. Your prospects come from:

- Your client (this may include internal candidates).

- Your client's board.

- Your database of candidates from similar searches.

- Networking contacts.

- Bespoke targeted research, as discussed in section III.

You've already had a successful benchmarking interview, which determined the exact critical skill and experience mix as well as what fit means to the client. Now it's time to start selling the project. In my experience, the best way to find the best qualified candidates with the highest potential interest in the least amount of time is to take the opportunity to them directly. In other words, I headhunt them.

Why Most Projects Fail at Recruiting the Best People

Unfortunately, many ESPs handle their first engagement with executive prospects poorly and are rejected out of hand. Too many recruiters confuse effectiveness with efficiency, using email and other forms of technology to quickly engage and qualify people—bypassing the personal touch that's really required at all levels, but especially at the executive level. This will quickly bring your carefully researched and constructed long list of several hundred prospects down to a handful. Now, it could be the right handful ... but you'll never know for sure: When you use an impersonal approach, you run the very real risk of rejecting the right candidate without even knowing it. Every person on your list deserves a phone call.

A-Courting We Shall Go

I'm a big believer in being direct. I started headhunting back in the early 1980s, when the term was still novel. Now most people understand what the term means, but back in the day the term was very descriptive of what we did. Long before email and LinkedIn, the number one way of introducing yourself to a prospect was via telephone. Before voicemail (oh, am I dating myself now), it could take many attempts to successfully connect with a prospective candidate. Often more than one message needed to be left with his or her executive assistants. Technology has made the job more efficient, but not necessarily as effective.

So, armed with your long list of prospects and a need for discretion, you need to personally call and talk to every one of them. When you get voicemail (which is all the time), leave them an intriguing message and private number with which to call you back. There are many ways to pitch an opportunity. If you're really interested in understanding what gets the attention of senior executives, we suggest you read *Pitch Anything: An Innovative Method for Presenting, Persuading, and Winning the Deal* by Oren Klaff. Oren's methodology for grabbing a senior executive's attention is unique, not the least bit smarmy, and can be learned by anyone. While the book's main focus is on getting an investor's time and attention during a formal presentation, the logic is transferable to a phone call. We are, after all, trying to grab the attention of a busy, fully-employed executive who is generating wealth at another company. They may be quite happy at the moment, and convincing them to speak with a total stranger about leaving their current employer can take some persuasion.

It's a tall order on a first phone call. This call often ends in a quick "No, thank you, I'm not looking," followed by a dial tone. I know, because I grew up in the recruiting business making calls like this in what was affectionately known as the "boiler room" with a half-dozen other guys. You really needed a thick skin to keep going. It took me about three weeks of constant rejection, despite memorizing dozens of snappy rebuttals, before I stopped to examine the process I'd been taught and came up with a more egalitarian approach. Within a short period of time I stopped cold calling entirely, and instead started warm calling. My career took off.

Let me explain, so you don't waste your time with methods most recruiters are taught but that haven't worked in decades.

Your sole objective in making initial contact with a prospect on your long list is to introduce yourself and get them to agree for you to send them the PP you so carefully crafted, to a confidential mail address of their choosing. Frequently, even if they have a few minutes to talk, I say, "I really don't want to speak with you now. I'd prefer to send you this information and then take a follow-up call from you after you've had 10 minutes of quiet uninterrupted time to review the material."

Thirty years later, my first contact with a prospect is always over the phone. Sometimes it takes a half-dozen calls or more but it's a small price to pay to reach a great candidate. (My personal record was 51 calls leaving 51 different voicemail messages before connecting with the CEO I was hunting at the time—well documented by the *Wall Street Journal* in an article nicknaming me "The Rogue Recruiter"). Your first contact with a prospect on your long list is always when you're the most vulnerable, because you're a complete stranger who's barged in to the executive's day unwanted. You need to create a peer relationship to have a fruitful discussion.

I've grown accustomed to being asked how I got their name—it's a fair question—and I always tell them they were identified by our research team as someone of high interest because ... (I fill in the "because" with the appropriate, honest answer). That's the way I start to gain their trust. Ninety-nine times out of 100 they'll give me a private email address and I politely request they stay on the line until I've sent the PP, to ensure it doesn't bounce back because of a typo.

Before I leave the call I tell them my name again, telephone number, and email address and invite them to look me up online at Perry-Martel's website. Then I tell them what happens next: that I know they're busy and appreciate they're not looking and don't have a current résumé, and emphasize that I don't want one—at least not now. If and when we speak in a few days (setting expectations here), it usually turns out they're interested in learning more. Many times

I'm asked to send the CCB too, but at this point it's premature and contains too much privileged information.

Lastly, I ask them when they'll have time to review the PP and when would be a good time for me to circle back, answer their questions, and gauge their interest. At no time do I engage them in further conversation, even if they want to. There's no point. If the research has been done correctly, I already know they can do the job. They have the skills and experience my client needs. The position profile will either pique their interest or not, and we need to understand why. The next time we speak it will be a conversation about them. The first phone call simply opens the door for a second call, which then becomes a discussion about them, their goals, and their career trajectory.

Positioning the Confidential Candidate Brief

My second call is much different. They've now accepted the PP, and it's up to me to turn them into a candidate or allow them to disengage. This is a critical inflection point in the process. Again, my call is designed to be low-key and unobtrusive. I'm not in sales mode. Rather, I'm still seeking to understand who they are as a person and leader, and what's important to them.

I start by asking them if they've had an opportunity to review the PP and if they have any immediate questions I can answer, or they'd prefer I call them back at another time. If they have questions, eventually they'll run out and begin to ask me what I'd like to know about them. I like intelligent questions, because then I know they're looking at the opportunity with a certain degree of real interest.

When it's my turn to ask questions I say, "I don't have any specific questions at the moment, but if you wouldn't mind: could you roll me back to when you were first getting out of college or university, and take me through your career up to now—if you have the time." Most do take the time, and I listen. Sometimes they talk almost continuously for as long as an hour, and I don't interrupt. At this juncture I'm not trying to qualify them but, rather, disqualify them. The question in my mind at this point is always: "Given what I know today about the client company and this role, is this candidate a good fit for them, and is my client's opportunity the next logical progression in this person's career?"

I listen very carefully because I'm interested. I listen because I need to understand what makes them tick, the types of challenges they rally for, the type of people they work best with—all the while relating everything back to the client's opportunity, and what we already know about the company's culture following the benchmark interview.

> While recruiting a senior vice-president for a multibillion-dollar real estate conglomerate, I suggested to the candidate over lunch that his son would have a much better chance of landing a hockey scholarship and being scouted for the National Hockey League (NHL) if the family lived in Chicago. That seemingly innocuous comment proved to be crucial in closing the deal. The candidate's employer made an outstanding counter offer, which I am certain to this day he would have taken had I not played the hockey card and thus included his family in the process.

What I'm Looking to Learn on the Qualifying Call

Because actions speak louder than words, the most important information you need to glean from this screening call and mini-interview has to do with their character, not their skill set. You already know from researching them that they're qualified technically.

We've found that character can be distilled from the patterns that reappear throughout their life. For our purposes, we're looking to discover if he or she has a strong *internal locus of control* or a strong *external locus of control*. You'll be able to assess this if you ask them to step you though their career story from the beginning to the present day.

"Somebody once said that in looking for people to hire, you look for three qualities: integrity, intelligence, and energy. And if you don't have the first, the other two will kill you." — *Warren Buffett, CEO*

I'm interested in the themes that appear throughout their career and:

- How they addressed controversy?

- How they took on new challenges?

- How their contribution positively impacted the organizations (or not!)?

The following explains how to do this unobtrusively. Actively *listen* to what the candidate says and how they're saying it. This goes beyond merely reflecting on the main points and summarizing what's been said. You need to listen beyond what's being said and get at the hidden meaning. You need to read (listen) between the lines. You must be genuinely attentive to the meaning and significance of what the person is saying. Show empathy. Use your emotional intelligence to pick up on the unspoken clues that hint at a larger story behind their words.

- Focus on the candidate's accomplishments. Did they grow as a result?

- Are they adaptable?

- Do they display natural resiliency?

- Listen to why each career move was made. In your head, ask yourself: Did it make sense?
  - Has there been steady career progression?
  - How clearly did they see the situation?
  - **Are they focused on execution?**
  - Progress: Are they making good decisions or are they making the same mistakes?
  - Was the candidate's decision reasonable?

- What are the driving forces in this person's career and life?

  - Are they ambitious?

  - Are they willing to take risks?

  - Look for personal situations that could influence performance.

- Determine areas of job satisfaction and dissatisfaction.

- Do the same things that were negatives in earlier situations exist in your company?

- What does the length of tenure at each company tell you?

  - Are there holes in their story? Note this for later referencing if they move forward in the process.

- Did they respond to situations in ways that will work in this specific situation and organization?

No Pain, No Gain?

Before I disengage I need to understand if their interest is more than casual and, if so, where it's coming from. A good salesperson knows that to make the sale you need to understand what motivates your prospect to buy. The process used for defining these motivational factors is what's referred to as "qualifying the buyer." As a recruiter, or ESP, I need to know what might motivate the candidate to leave his or her current position and join my client's organization. Strategically, these motivational factors normally fall into two categories: pain factors and gain factors.

Pain factors are any issues in the candidate's current job or work environment with which he or she is not totally satisfied. These issues push the candidate away from their employer and might cause them to look elsewhere. Gain factors, on the other hand—as you may have already gathered—are any attractive elements they read about in the PP or discovered while talking with you.

Understand as best you can both the pain and gain factors early in the interview by asking one or more of the following questions.

To Establish Pain Factors

Here are two quick questions I ask to understand what may motivate someone to move:

1. The satisfaction question goes like this: "(Name of the person), obviously if you were totally satisfied at the ABC Company, we wouldn't be talking here today. What are some of the factors in your current work situation with which you're not completely satisfied? Why are these important to you?"

2. The grass is greener question is asked this way: "(Name of the person), what are some of the factors you'd hope to find in a new employment situation that aren't present in your current work situation, and why are these important to you?"

To Establish Gain Factors

And these are two innocuous questions I ask to understand what may attract them to your opportunity:

1. The authority question: "(Name of the person), what are some of the factors that motivated you to come and talk with us today? What do you find attractive in the opportunity?"

2. The futures question: "What was there about the description of the mandate at (name of the client) that most interested you?" (Followed by asking for anything else that was interesting to him or her.)

When you get the CCB back, you can see if those factors are reflected in their answers. If they factor in heavily then you're finally beginning to understand what it may take to keep them interested and engaged as you go through your interview process. It may also give you insight as to how to craft an offer and a deal. When you now know what's driving their engagement, you can advise others who may interview the candidate later what needs to be emphasized. This will substantially improve your ability to land the candidate you choose.

These motivational factors also will come in handy later, when you make an employment offer. Any good offer strategy will include discussion reinforcing the idea that these important needs can be met in your work environment. This adds a certain amount of additional value that the candidate should find quite appealing if he or she elects to join your organization.

CLOSING ON THE FIRST FACE-TO-FACE INTERVIEW

If we think there's enough of a match, then we offer to send them the CCB to complete in lieu of a résumé. In order to set expectations and end our conversation on a cordial note, I explain the next steps going forward:

- I indicate that our meeting face-to-face is now being driven by his responsiveness.

- That until the candidate says so, his or her decision to move forward and investigate the opportunity will not be revealed to our client.

Behind the Scenes

As soon as the individual indicates they'll complete the CCB they become a candidate, and we open a file on them. As the search progresses and they're invited to continue in the process, their file will grow. We not only file our notes and impressions following every interaction, but also link to articles and other sources of information relevant to their candidacy. Technology-wise we accomplish this using a software program called Invenias. Invenias was designed by Executive Search Professionals for use by Executive Search Professionals. One of its best features is its ability to let me produce very detailed reports for our clients.

TRADECRAFT

As much as I appreciate my iPhone, iPad, and the Internet, I'm an old-school guy when it comes to making connections with people. Don't get me wrong: I do try everything new when it comes out. I have beta tested more software and gear than anyone I know. I'm a voracious reader on everything recruiting, marketing, sales, and leadership related. I have hundreds of HR-related books and journals. However, the main tools I rely on are:

- POTS—plain old telephone system.

- ZoomInfo.com—reliable data source.

- Invenias—a software solution built specifically for the executive search and strategic recruitment sector.

- ExecuNet—online community for senior executives.

- LinkedIn—research and publishing platform.

While accessing executives has become more challenging because of technology, my day-to-day life has become more manageable because of the simplicity and interoperability of these tools. Watch this quick demo on ZoomInfo now on your smartphone to get a better idea of what I mean (Figure 4.6).

Figure 4.6   QR code - How to ZoomInfo.
Source: www.zoominfo.com/business/products/zoominfo-pro.

NOTES

1. http://en.wikipedia.org/wiki/Automatic_summarization.
2. https://www.domo.com/blog/2013/08/ceos-of-americas-largest-companies-embracing-twitter-and-linkedin-facebook-not-so-much/.
3. www.ft.com/cms/s/0/19975256-1af2-11de-8aa3-0000779fd2ac.html#axzz3g5hRckz7.
4. www.businessinsider.in/Why-half-of-all-new-executives-fail-can-be-narrowed-down-to-4-reasons/articleshow/46436468.cms.
5. http://navalent.s3.amazonaws.com/rtp_exec_summary_vf3_140916.pdf.

CHAPTER 5

Finding the Right Fit

Lions Don't Need to Roar

After all, the ultimate goal of all research is not objectivity, but truth.
—Helene Deutsch

Michael and I flew to Milwaukee for the first interviews: Our race to find candidates was over, but the search was still just beginning. We'd combined the "fit" and "face-to-face" interviews to save time for Carl, the Search Chair, and to complete the personal fit portion we hoped to present several dissimilar candidates. It was going to be a busy few days.

At a first interview I have a limited agenda. By this point, Michael and I have already reviewed their résumés and completed Confidential Candidate Briefs (CCBs). We've both talked with them by telephone. Each candidate had passed our preliminary screening. On paper, they're well qualified. Next I want to sell the opportunity while assessing their character.

To understand each candidate as a person we need to understand their story. At a core level, I want to understand their dominant locus of control: Is it internal or external? Listening to their story will give me strong clues. Michael sits next to me on the plane while we review the follow-up questions and decide which of us will interview which candidate while the other takes notes.

Having arrived at our hotel I immediately confirm my arrangements with the front desk manager for refreshments to be at hand for our guests, then head to our conference room to set up. As we only have one meeting today I made a mental note to try the gym and pool later.

After greeting our first guest and listening to his advice on places to go in Milwaukee, we dove right in. I always begin interviews the same, asking, "Please, take me back to when you were graduating from college or university, and take me through your career, ending with why we're sitting here today." Then I sit back and I listen. I'm encouraged now and again because of perfunctory pauses in the candidate's story to uncover dates and times, and the names of accomplices. I will remember to use this information later, if and when I'm checking their references. Michael sits across from me, furiously writing. Soon enough, though, it'll be his turn to lead the interview and my time to scribe.

The hotel is nice and Michael's great to travel with. Perhaps it was working together for two years before joining forces, or maybe he was just that insightful—regardless, he was a natural for the business. At the end of each session we recapped what we now knew about each candidate. What were the defining moments in his or her career? How did he or she handle pressure and challenges? What types of situations seemed to bring out the best in him or her? What are his or her dominant character traits? As for raw intelligence: Is he or she book smart or street smart? I'm hoping for both, in most cases.

I always map the candidate's story against the situation he or she is facing, my client's foibles, and the new opportunity. But mostly I'm out to discover if the candidate is the master of his or her own destiny, to the extent that that's possible. Does he or she have a strong external locus of control or a strong internal locus of control? The assessment of his or her story is always about what's best for the client first, and what's also in line with the individual's wants, needs, and desires. I'm also assessing whether he or she has a strong self-concept or is completely narcissistic.

Fast forward a little. We'd been interviewing for two days now and the candidates were great, but I was still looking for a COO that was, or had been, for lack of a better term, a "shop rat." I was hoping to meet someone who'd started on the shop floor and advanced through the ranks, taking on ever more responsibility with each promotion, but who also had "executive presence." Our eyes were peeled for someone who had taken chances, learned from their mistakes, shared credit with others, and accepted blame when things went wrong. Humility is unexpected, but refreshing.

In the back of my mind was the story Fred had told us about emigrating from postwar Poland. He left, with his lovely bride and little else, just before the Berlin Wall was erected and the Iron Curtain descended on Eastern Europe. Fred settled in Los Angeles and began working as a maintenance engineer at a small tool-and-die company, which he eventually bought and turned into a thriving business. Fred is a character and well-loved by his employees. The soon-to-be chief operating officer needed to gain his trust and respect fast if he was to be successful and eventually transition into the CEO role. The successful candidate needed to speak Fred's language.

At the end of our time in Milwaukee I liked two candidates: Dave and Jim. Dave was a solid guy with the right experience and good leadership skills. His being less seasoned than several of the other candidates was my only reservation.

And then there was Jim.

Jim rang all the right bells during our interview for many reasons. He struck me as the "what you see is what you get" type. He wasn't trying to put on a dog-and-pony show. While Michael was afraid he didn't want it bad enough—that he wasn't going to sell himself in the interview—my view was that we hadn't yet provided enough information about the opportunity to make him jump up and down with excitement. And frankly, at this stage, I wanted a conversation with him—not a show.

The guy that Michael liked best, I hated. It happens! This candidate's education and experience were spot-on, but he moved jobs too much for my liking. He was also dressed to impress. The cut of his suit said so. His clothes were meant for the boardroom, his language laden with so many pop psychology and business buzzwords it made my eyes roll. His demeanor didn't fit on the shop floor, and he was a name-dropper—where he went to school, who he went to school with, who was a member of his country club, that kind of thing. It was all well-rehearsed and designed to impress. He kept tapping his Northwestern ring on the table as we talked, and that really annoyed the crap out of me. Other than that, though, he was perfect: He looked every bit the part of an executive, and he certainly spoke like a typical MBA grad.

Michael and I interviewed all seven candidates over two-and-a-half days, comparing notes all the while. Like barristers arguing over a case we vetted each candidate on their merits. It was clear that several of the candidates had changed jobs involuntarily, which in and of itself is insignificant as a lone event, but if it's happened more than once or twice, and for the same reason, or given the same circumstances, then you have to question whether it's a habit or character flaw. Either way, it's a problem.

In the end we eliminated four of the group of seven. As the lead ESP, I would now be responsible for moving ahead with the three remaining candidates. Going forward the interview team would now consist of just myself and Carl (the Search Chair). Mark (Haluska, the creator of the CCB whom we introduced back in Chapter 3) would continue digging for other candidates as people were eliminated, because at the end of the day people aren't products; they have free will and can stay or go as they please.

THE IMPORTANCE OF PLANNING

There's no single faster way to snatch defeat from the jaws of victory than through thoughtlessness. I hope the following absolutely true story never, ever happens to you or your company:

> Back in the late '90s I was asked to finish a search project another firm had been unable to complete for more than a year. The company, a large technology multinational, had been trying to recruit a president for their office in Japan.
>
> Within four days our head researcher had identified, qualified, and contacted the president of this client's major competitor's country manager in Japan. (This still stands as a record more than 15 years later). On paper the executive seemed ideal for the role. After speaking with Hiroshi for several hours the following week, and justifying why the client spent $6,000 to fly him to their North American head office for a face-to-face interview, I was now picking him up at the airport.
>
> The 14-hour flight didn't appear to have taken much of a toll on Hiroshi, so I took him directly to his hotel and we went for a quick bite to eat at a neighboring outdoor market. Over dinner (breakfast for Hiroshi) we discussed the business at hand and schedule for tomorrow, which I'd mapped out with the client's HR director.
>
> After sitting patiently in the general reception area of the client's head office for a half-hour past the appointment time, we were invited by an executive assistant to wait in the senior executive vice-president's boardroom. We waited unattended for another twenty minutes or more because he was apparently running late. When the hiring manager finally arrived he quickly introduced himself, extending his arm for the perfunctory handshake. He then plopped down in his chair, casually leafing through the briefing file I'd couriered to him the previous week.
>
> Half-looking up from his reading, the senior executive vice-president asked my candidate, "How old are you?"

"Sixty-eight," Hiroshi replied.

"Oh," said the client in a startled manner. Then, without pausing: "We were hoping for someone younger. No matter. Where should we begin?"

You can't make this stuff up.

The interview went downhill quickly from there, careening toward disaster with each successive insensitive question uttered by my client. It was obvious to me the hiring manager hadn't read the in-depth report we'd provided on cultural idioms peculiar to Japan, nor was he following the carefully scripted interview guide we'd provided. I later learned the HR director had decided, on her own, to let him wing it. She was uncomfortable suggesting anything different. It was my bad for not anticipating that.

Although I had allowed this uncomfortable situation to happen, a couple important lessons weren't lost on me that day which I'll come back to later in this section. First, though, I need to explain why an old truism is absolutely critical when recruiting an executive:

You only get one opportunity to make a good first impression.

A vital component to hiring greatness is your interview plan. Yes, I said *plan*: From the first moment you connect with an executive your actions are under scrutiny, so it's important to present a positive image. Remember, nearly 100 percent of the time your target candidate already has a great job. They're happy and productive. There's a good chance that they don't *need* you or your opportunity. The type of people you want are at the top of their game and your approach will be just the latest in the previous hundreds, if not thousands, of calls to which these in-demand executives have already responded.

Without a specific plan of attack you'll quickly find most executives have a very strong "I'd rather fight than switch" muscle. While you may be resolute and willing to go the extra mile to close the deal, the object of your desire simply isn't interested. They are, however, interested in that concept we introduced in a previous chapter—the "what's in it for me" factor, or WIFM. People familiar with Toastmasters International, the public speaking organization, understand that the most reliable way to hold an audience's attention to deliver an effective message is to understand and leverage their WIFM.

If you intend to recruit world-class talent you need an awesome, WIFM-infused plan: one that exploits the latest and greatest intelligence from the eclectic disciplines of marketing, sales, project management, and human psychology. That's what you'll take away from this section of the book: a better methodology and process for talent-scouting the best executives in the world. Apply these ideas to guide your executive searches and you'll consistently locate, evaluate, and attract the precise executives you need to help your company soar.[1]

Before we talk about interview plans, though, I'd like to explain how spending a little "psychic cash" to put your best foot forward can help you achieve your ultimate objective of hiring greatness.

INTERVIEW ETIQUETTE—PUTTING YOUR BEST FOOT FORWARD

Pause for a moment to consider where we are in the story: As a client, you've invested thousands of dollars to come up with a short list of candidates who can help your organization reach new heights. A Search Committee has been assembled to ensure a balanced and fair assessment of each candidate, captained by a Search Chair tasked with keeping the process moving.

Taking the above into account, and assuming that attracting the very best executive is important, it's now absolutely essential to come up with a robust and consistent interview process. The process must produce the executive hire you want *and* provide a positive experience to the candidates—especially if they've spent 14 hours on a plane the night before, and are now interviewing in a diametrically opposed time zone.

The "why" should be obvious. Let's focus instead on the "how."

Conceptually, this is simple: You should treat the interview much like a first date. This is a business meeting of equals who both have much to gain. Both parties need to make a positive first impression. Your initial research may target 10, 20, or 50 or more prospective candidates. I say "prospective" because they aren't really candidates unless they agree to your interview program—they may, however, also be prospective customers who could be in a position to buy or recommend your company's product or service in the future. This is not a simple employment transaction without consequences for those companies and individuals who execute poorly.

As we've said, the candidates that firms really want have options—frequently, lots of options. So when these candidates seriously consider places they'd like to work, they'll typically rank them in their heads from best to worst. This is a game of winner take all: The candidate will go with his or her first choice, with no prizes for coming in second. But all the firms seriously considered occupy a share of the candidate's mind, and how that candidate is treated ultimately impacts the brand equity he or she assigns to the firm.

The consequences of this should be obvious because great candidates often take jobs in the same industry. They may even be the firm's future potential customers or strategic partners. So how they perceive their treatment by the firms in their consideration can positively or negatively impact their behaviors, either through word of mouth or, in some instances, choosing to work with the firm in the future.

Friend and author Timothy Keiningham, author of *The Wallet Allocation Rule: Winning the Battle for Share* (largely considered the gold standard in customer loyalty and customer engagement thinking), recently shared this powerful story with me:

> I was speaking at a university event to a group of alumni, and one of the people there who had graduated many decades earlier shared an experience where he punished a firm that he felt hadn't treated him well in the interview process. He had graduated from college as a chemist, and applied for a job with a large firm. While he could accept that he wasn't qualified for the position, the way he was treated left him feeling snubbed. As a result, in his new job he made a point of designing the specifications for their products so that it would specifically exclude that firm from being able to work with them. As a result, the treatment of one person in the interview process cost that firm significant business for decades.

While this is clearly an extreme example of the ripple effect of a bad interview, it serves as a stark warning. The candidates you interview will be ambassadors and, often, customers of your firm. So it's imperative to treat them in a way that will reflect positively on your brand regardless of whether or not they're offered a position with the firm.

Unfortunately, many companies fail miserably at this despite the zillions spent carefully crafting their brand. But you can avoid this fatal gaffe by simply treating every candidate the same way you might indulge the CEO of your largest corporate client. After all, in all probability you need this person as much as they need you. Now is *not* the time to play "Mohammed to the mountain," as so many companies do. The company (of course) views itself as the mountain.

How you treat a prospective candidate from the second they arrive until departure will leave a lasting impression, one that will do more to help negotiate a final deal than anything else—including money. You can easily make it a positive experience. After all, letting the wrong person slip through your fingers at this point may cause irreparable damage to your company's future. It certainly did for my client I mentioned earlier, whose boorish SVP had taken the interview off-script with disastrous consequences. This client couldn't understand why the candidate—*to whom my client incidentally made an offer on the spot*—was now not even remotely interested in joining the firm. The following day I returned to the client's office to explain how I thought future interviews should be conducted, but the SVP's complete lack of interest in improving his interviewing skills forced me to terminate the relationship and return the retainer.

Several months later the company filled the position. Their new search firm convinced the company to hire a Korean national as president to oversee the branch offices in Japan, Korea, and Vietnam. We'll never know if the company was just oblivious to the cultural differences between the three countries, or if something larger was in play. We do know, however, that the firm's Japan revenues plummeted the following year from US$158 million to less than US$11 million. Within 18 months the firm was purchased for billions less than its former value. (The HR director moved down the street to a multibillion-dollar corporation shortly after the sale, oblivious to her part in the company's undoing.)

HOW TO SHAPE A ROBUST INTERVIEW PROCESS

What is a robust interviewing process? It actually starts well before the interviews ever begin and, though it can be defined in a variety of ways, some main points are listed below:

Before the Interview

First, send an itinerary to the candidate's home address by FedEx or express mail immediately after all interview plans have been arranged. Using their home address is particularly important if the individual is currently employed, since it eliminates the risk of an email being opened at work. [Fact: Most companies now (legally) monitor email for violations of no-compete agreements or to see who is loyal, who might be looking, and therefore who is next to be let go.]

- An itinerary is always needed but is especially important if there's travel involved. In addition to covering all travel arrangements, if any, let the candidate know in advance the time, date, and venue of the meeting. In terms of actual meeting location, be cognizant about candidates being in public or high-traffic areas as employees or clients may recognize this person and compromise their confidentiality.

- Tell candidates the name of the individual who will greet them upon their arrival, the name and title of who will conduct the interview(s), and what format the interview will take. Indicate how long the interview is likely to be and what information you'll cover. If the interview involves the Search Committee, make certain all members have a copy of the itinerary to avoid any confusion.

Second, if more than one individual will be involved with the interview, educate all members of the interview panel on how to be an ambassador for the company. Your very first meeting should be scripted, in a manner of speaking. We all think and perceive situations differently, and what one member of the team may deem acceptable may not be consistent with what other team members believe creates a welcoming atmosphere.

- Whether the process entails a single or several interviews, one of the first things the Search Committee should agree upon is a realistic and targeted time frame in which consensus will be achieved. This is critical in the final stages of the process when you could be in danger of losing both your first and second choices for the position if assurances of timely feedback are not kept.

- Although it's impossible to plan for every contingency, if the Search Committee will be involved with the interviews be mindful of prior commitments such as meetings, required travel, and vacation schedules. Rescheduling a "first date," when it could have been avoided in the first place, does not bode well for an optimum first impression.

- If the single interview or series of interviews is going to go for several hours, be sure to schedule regular breaks as nature does have a way of calling at the most inconvenient times.

Third, go over the candidate's complete résumé and CCB, if provided. As the candidate advances to meet the next level of interviewers, ask every interviewer to record their answers to the following questions:

- What has the candidate accomplished that's *relevant* to the company's goals?

- How does his or her experience meet your needs?

- Is the candidate's story credible and convincing?

Lastly, your candidate should be promptly greeted by a member of the Search Committee or even the chairperson. Whoever is assigned to greet the candidate should also introduce them to everyone participating in the interview.

Prior to the interview, it's imperative that everyone involved has meticulously reviewed the candidate's résumé and any other materials provided such as white papers, articles, presentations, interview notes that accompany the candidates file, etc. Make certain that, as the interviews progress, you have questions prepared to address any areas that may require clarification.

Expect your ESP to brief you on the candidate's interests, concerns, and fit. Expect your consultant to identify where the candidate might be shy on relevant experience and why you should interview them. Your consultant should—at a minimum—provide you with ongoing feedback after debriefing both the candidate and interviewers. Any issues or concerns that arise must be acted upon for resolution along the way.

As part of your "sale" to candidates, you should also have other information available for them to read either there or to take home with them. It has been our experience that most executives, once past the initial meetings with recruiting staff, will already have downloaded and reviewed any publicly available news and reports such as your company's 10-K Report, 10-Q Report, 8-K, Proxy Statement, Schedule 13D, and Form 144.

What they won't have access to, but may be very interested in personally, are internal newsletters or any comparative studies you may want to share for strategic reasons. If the candidate will need to relocate, you should proactively provide the candidate with updated information from the Chamber of Commerce on the local community and housing.

A word of caution: I would think twice about hiring any executive who hasn't reviewed those company documents and financial statements in detail before their final interviews. On the candidate's part, they are about to make a multimillion-dollar investment in their career by joining your firm and I would expect them to execute proper due diligence. Failure to do so could be a sign of carelessness.

Closing the First Interview and Subsequent Interviews

Irrespective of how many interviews you hold, timely follow-up is crucial with those individuals still under consideration and even those eliminated from contention. If the Search Committee has agreed upon a target time frame to reach consensus and set follow-up interviews (as they should have done in the planning stages), there shouldn't be a problem clearly communicating when the candidates will be contacted. Of course, you must then strictly adhere to your stipulated response time frame. Not doing so shows a lack of interest or organization on your part.

During interviews, watch closely and take notes. You're not looking for perfection, but in general you want to know if the candidates are:

- Prepared?

- Convincing?

- Credible?

- Logical?

- Compelling?

Along with how well do they:

- Handle pressure?

- Think on their feet?

- Make use of the English language?

If you hired a consultant then this is his or her job. It's critical that the consultant follows through on this, since you'll have to live with the consequences. (This is all the more reason to ensure that the consultant uses a contact management system like Invenias.) Expect the ESP to send you a report detailing how each meeting was concluded with each candidate. This will help ensure that the money marketing invests in building your positive corporate image is not carelessly tarnished by the ESP forgetting to follow through with all candidates during the interview process.

THE QUICK AND THE DEAD

They used to say there were just two types of people in the Old West (and by "Old West" I mean the job market): the quick and the dead. The quick knew that it came down to not only talent and ideas, but execution, while the dead thought only talent mattered—with predictable results.

"Moore's Law" predicted the raw processing and storage capacity that has made the Internet possible and taken us into an electronically connected world. Today people are connected not only to each other but also each other's knowledge. It's said that beginning in the year 2010 the cumulative codified knowledge of the world began to double every 11 hours (in 1975 it was every seven years). The insight you have at night will be outdated by daybreak. The shelf life of knowledge will soon be the same as that of a banana.

So the long-term value of specific knowledge has taken a nosedive. Knowledge is still power, but the longevity of that power has been dramatically reduced. This means that *we now work in a world in which the opportunities available to us, and our organizations, are growing exponentially*—and because everyone is connected to knowledge, everyone is connected to the opportunities that knowledge provides. If your company isn't pursuing the opportunities and competitive advantage contained in this exponentially growing and knowledge-based world then, rest assured, somewhere in the world one of your competitors surely is.

> *"One of the most effective ways of creating new knowledge is for two or more people to combine their existing knowledge to produce something entirely new. This is the basis of creative thinking. Mix existing pieces of knowledge over heated and excited discussion and there is no telling what will emerge."*
> —Ron Wiens, author, *Building Organizations that Leap Tall Buildings in a Single Bound*

Competitive advantage today lies in an organization's ability to exploit this explosion of knowledge and see the opportunities before anyone else. Those companies that can consistently do this faster than their competitors will thrive and prosper, while the others wither and die.

Back when the machine was the center of a typical organization's universe, the role of management was to surround their machines with procedures employees must do to serve the machine. But in a knowledge-based society, it's human innovation that creates competitive advantage, value, and wealth: One need look no further than Apple, Facebook, or Uber to see proof of this on a daily basis.

Today, management's job is to surround their people with an environment that gets them working and building together, an atmosphere that promotes the leveraging of the creativity and knowledge of others to constantly acquire, build, and productize new knowledge. There are three things managers and their leaders need to do, and do well, to build such an environment.

The first is to help their people believe in themselves. In today's winning organizations, the employees themselves take things to new places. They are the ones trying new things. They are the ones making mistakes, learning from these mistakes, and moving on (for example, Disney and Google). When they get stuck or go off into the weeds, the employees of these winning organizations are the first to recognize it and freely put up their hands for help. The degree to which people believe in themselves is a measure of your organization's Emotional Intelligence (EI).

The second is to build an organization where people care about each other. How can caring produce a winning bottom line? The answer was most eloquently articulated by Jean Autry, former CEO of the Publisher Group, when he said "I need to know that you care before I care to know what you know." Caring is the basis of trust. If I know that you care about me and my success then I can trust you. If I can trust you, I can speak openly and frankly with you. If I can speak openly and frankly with you, we can solve problems together. And if we can solve problems together, we can leverage each other's creativity and knowledge to build competitive advantage (for example, Pixar and Apple). The ability of its people to trust is a measure of your organization's Relationship Intelligence (RI).

The third is to instill "common cause." In winning organizations employees have a deep and common understanding of the organization's desired future. But not only do they understand the organization's goals and objectives, they believe in them (for example, Cisco and Starbucks). Achieving these goals is personally meaningful. The strength of attachment of your people to your desired future is a measure of your organization's Corporate Intelligence (CI).

More than ever, companies today need leaders capable of engaging a community of people with a common mission and who are willing to routinely operate at levels of peak performance. This has deep implications for whom you hire, which aptitudes and qualities you recruit, and how you lead. Skillfully combining EI, RI, and CI produces leadership equity: a situation where employees are plugged in, turned on, and in tune with your organization. When this happens, you've got the organizational equivalent of the Triple Crown of thoroughbred racing.

Increasing company value isn't just about collecting talented people, though. It's also about aligning them with the company's overall strategy—getting them to buy in and to commit to a common vision. Most importantly, it's about compelling them to work toward an idea not because you told them to, but because you've given them passionate reasons to do it. That's how organizations compete profitably in a knowledge-based economy as centers of excellence, without leaving dead bodies at every gunfight.

THE FIVE PILLARS OF SUCCESS

During the course of more than 50 collective years in the executive search and recruiting business and more than 100,000 interviews, Mark and I have observed that it is far more important that a leadership candidate possess specific intangible core attributes, than just decades of industry experience.

These core attributes go far beyond mere technical skills. They are what allow some people to produce at a superhuman pace while others grow weary after eight hours. If this notion seems contrary to logic, look at the facts: Through the ages, profiles of successful high-performance people reveal that their most important competencies had little to do with skills (Carnegie/Rockefeller), training (Gates/Jobs), or work experience (Dell/Cuban), but rather with their mindset (Welch/Churchill). Indeed, we all know people who can produce a week's worth of results in a six-hour day.

Contrary to popular belief, leaders aren't born. They develop over time and perfect their skills, slowly becoming expert through experience.[2] For more thinking on this read "The Making of an Expert" by K. Anders Ericsson, Michael J. Prietula, and Edward T. Cokely in the July–August 2007 *Harvard Business Review*.

Based on our observations, Mark, myself, and others have worked to identify a baseline of 28 core attributes we've seen in successful executives.[3] These core attributes have been grouped into five categories, or "pillars of success," as we refer to them internally (see Figure 5.1). Every executive candidate you consider should be assessed against these five pillars. Beware: From our experience, these core attributes are fully present in less than one percent of the adult population.

But if you specifically design your interviews to uncover these core attributes, while holding the candidate's skills and experience as a constant, you will hire a superior executive and your team will be

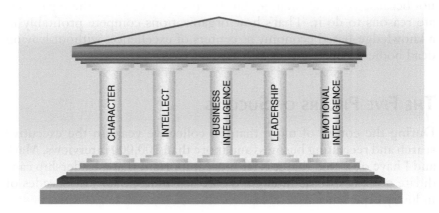

Figure 5.1   Five pillars of success.

closer to achieving your organization's full potential. As you make your way through the interviewing process, work with your ESP and vice-president of HR to construct interview questions that assess potential candidates against these attributes.

The 28 Core Attributes

Character

1. Integrity, honesty, credibility, and trust—What degree of integrity and credibility does the candidate have among peers, the industry, the news media, Wall Street, and investors? (Honesty and trust are binary attributes—they either have them or they don't. Watch for inconsistencies throughout the interviews, and reference check for this attribute thoroughly.)

2. Persistence—Is the candidate an assertive individual who will execute programs to successful fruition? Is the professional highly self-motivated or an order-taker in disguise?

3. Resiliency—Has the candidate shown, by his or her actions and deeds, that he or she has an ability to take a hit (*personally or in business*) and keep moving forward or does he or she fold

early in a battle and hide behind "market conditions?" Listen very carefully to his or her story in the first and second interviews, and make certain they match. Examine the indicators closely because this is a pattern they'll repeat throughout their life.

4. Personal Mindset—Does the candidate view the glass as half-empty or half-full?[4]

5. Judgment Calls—Does the candidate have a track record of sound judgment calls in a variety of different business situations?

6. Battle Scars—Does he or she have substantial management experience, and an understanding of the factors that make a business work?

7. Naturally Inquisitive—Does he or she have a love of continuous learning? What has the candidate been interested enough in personally to follow or contribute to steadily for more than a decade?

Intellect

8. Strategy: Market Driving—Where has the candidate shown the ability to capture and define a business strategy beyond the original product/ concept, and then garner the support of stakeholders?

9. Enterprising Thought Process—Does the candidate think in an enterprising way? Do they come up with one hundred ideas to find the two, highly creative and strategic concepts that can propel their company to new heights, or has their ability to think been limited by rigid policies while working with other companies? Can they transfer that behavior or attitude to your organization?

10. Problem Solving—Does the candidate have intellectual and intuitive problem-solving skills?

11. Smart—Do they have a strong intellect, coupled with pragmatism and common sense? The candidate's personal verbal communications skills are a good indication.

12. Analytical—Does the candidate typically look for multiple variables? When problem solving, do they often fold in concepts and attributes that make others stretch to understand the bigger picture? Do they know what they don't know? Probe for evidence they've recognized this in the past, and ask how they filled the gap.

Business Intelligence

13. Judgment—Does the candidate have the ability to deal with novel, complex situations where there is no corporate history or industry road map?

14. Business Knowledge—Is the candidate genuinely immersed in the guts of the business? How have they woven themselves into the fabric of the industry? Is their knowledge superficial or is it extensive enough to allow them to provide superior counsel? Likewise, are their relations with business leaders deep and meaningful or shallow and opportunistic?

15. Cash Conscious—Does the candidate understand the critical importance of cash to emerging companies? Do they watch the dollar and time expenditures as an entrepreneur would, or simply spend and manage knowing the paycheck and benefits will come no matter what?

16. Risk Tolerance—Does the person have the courage to meet stiff challenges? Do they assume risk comfortably, or simply play it safe?

17. Customer Focused—Do they understand how markets work? Where have they demonstrated their ability to get appropriate products/service to your type of customer? Explore how their regular management regime reinforces this to the organization.

Leadership

18. Commitment—Where and when has the candidate already demonstrated a built-in, unrelenting drive to succeed?

19. Passion—Is the candidate genuinely passionate about your industry and your company? Can they identify with your "Why?" (as Simon Sinek would say).[5]

20. People Skills—Does the candidate have an ability to hire and fire quickly, manage effectively, and blend together the intricate personalities and quirks of talented people? Do they always seem to be looking for talent so that when that perfect opportunity arises, the ideal candidate is already waiting in the wings?

21. Visionary Capabilities—Does the candidate bring vision to the direction of the company? Where they have demonstrated that they have the ability to deliver ideas/programs that bring immediate value is important, but so too is their ability to plot a course for the future and influence people to follow.

22. Proactive—Does the candidate's approach to their responsibilities embody a forward-thinking, proactive mindset or simply the aim to hide behind his or her title, reacting to situations if and when necessary?

23. Entrepreneurial/Intrapreneurial—Does the candidate watch dollar and time expenditures like an entrepreneur, just as if he/she owned the company?

24. Focus on Results—Has the candidate demonstrated an ability to recruit a quality subordinate team, to generate high levels of performance from team members, and get them to work together?

Emotional Intelligence

25. Self-Concept—Is the candidate's self-concept healthy and strong enough to navigate treacherous waters intuitively, as well as develop and motivate staff as though the staff developed the ideas themselves?[6]

26. Culture—Does the candidate by dint of personal style and experience establish a core philosophy of operation (a value set) and organizational culture that will promote the desired results?

27. Empathy—Does the candidate have the ability to connect with employees and customers?

28. Commitment—Is there a demonstrated willingness to make a substantial personal commitment of time to the people in the business?

Emotional intelligence is critical to success in an executive role today. More than ever before, the command and control structures and authoritarian dictates of management have little effect on knowledge workers other than to point them toward greener pastures with more enlightened leadership. For this reason, we strongly suggest you incorporate EI assessments in your hiring practices. For example, when we've narrowed a search field to three candidates or less, we request they each complete an EQ-I assessment (see Figure 5.2).

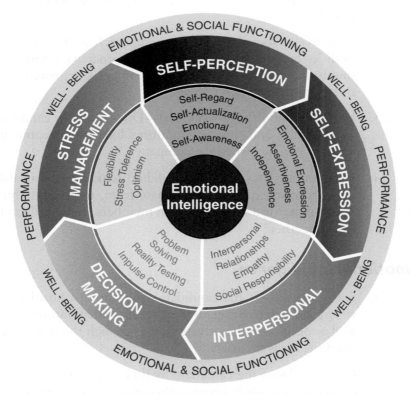

Figure 5.2   EQ-I assessment.

At Perry-Martel we've used the *BarOn EQ-I Leadership Report*[7] for more than a decade. This report examines EQ-I results as they relate to leadership skills. The report's results can be used for the general assessment of leadership strengths and weaknesses to assist in leadership selection, placement, and development decisions. It's important to note that weaknesses may contribute to ineffective leadership, and even derailment. The assessment is applicable to most levels and functions of leadership, be they at the executive, management, or operational levels. Empirical research (based in part on leadership theory) while developing the report involving thousands of leaders worldwide demonstrated that effective leadership must embrace the organization's culture, which includes both people and processes.

Creating behavioral interview questions to assess the candidate's attributes in these areas is something your HR people can help with and an expertise they'll be happy to demonstrate. But it's important to note that this type of interview isn't a replacement for the EQ-I assessment. Rather, they complement each other. Ultimately the assessment can be used to validate your references, thus providing an extra layer of reassurance.

FOUR COMMON FAILURES TO AVOID

Have you heard the term "empty suit"? It describes an executive who doesn't know what he or she is doing, and Enron wasn't the first and won't be the last company to fall victim to this virus. For this reason it's important to be aware of the superficial evaluation factors most likely to affect your perception of a candidate. Thankfully, a fair amount of research has been done on what encourages interviewers to hire the candidates they do. We've reviewed these factors extensively in all three editions of *Guerrilla Marketing for Job Hunters*, and have gone to great lengths to teach job hunters how to leverage that knowledge.

Let me expound on these superficial evaluation factors by recapping a study highlighted in *Work Rules! Insights from Inside Google to Transform How You Live and Lead* by Laszlo Bock, senior vice-president of people operations at Google. The book contains insight that should be noted by even the casual interviewer. Bock discusses the implications of snap hiring decisions based on first impressions, concluding that typical interviews are a waste of time because 99.4 percent of the time is spent trying to confirm whatever impression the interviewer formed in the first 10 seconds.[8]

Bock then reviews a study by Frank Schmidt and John Hunter published in the 1998 *Psychological Bulletin* of the American Psychological Association,[9] examining the metadata of 85 years of research on how well assessments actually predict performance. They examined 19 different assessment techniques and found that typical, unstructured job interviews were pretty bad at predicting how someone would perform once hired.

The most interesting finding, for me, was the confirmation that:

- Unstructured interviews could explain only 14 percent of an employee's performance;

- Reference checks explain 7 percent;

- Years of experience 3 percent; and

- The best predictor was giving the candidate a job-related task to complete, at 29 percent.[10]

We'll show you how to use this knowledge to your advantage later in this section, when we detail how you take your finalist candidates for a "test drive." First, though, I want to point out a few typical land mines.

Here are the four common failures to avoid: Bear in mind that there are always exceptions, but it's wise to stay on high alert. Whenever Mark and I "fall in love" with a candidate we force ourselves to take a healthy step back and figure out why we feel so strongly. This is to ensure we're not being biased by the following prejudices:

1. Charm—Outward personality is never an accurate predictor of success in any role—we'll discuss the Bernie Madoffs of the world later in the book. Probe for substance, and ignore the width of the candidate's smile. Many of the most successful leaders we have met would best be described as "detached."

2. Industry Experience—Depending on the size of the company and its growth stage, sophisticated knowledge of your product

may not be critical. Make your decision on the basis of a broad range of factors, not only on industry experience. Product knowledge can be bought (in a VP of product management, for example), whereas baseline success characteristics cannot. You either have them or you don't.

3. Pedigree—Prestigious school credentials are nice to have. They may even come with a built-in network, but that won't guarantee success. Keep the candidate's credentials in proper context and vet them fully before making an offer. If you need B-school contacts, consider adding them at the board level or form an advisory group or panel of experts. Look at what may already be available through LinkedIn's Groups.

4. "Golden Boy" references—By this we mean references from people who have worked indirectly or consulted for a candidate but didn't directly work for or with them. If a reference can't say "I remember when they did…," discount their flattery heavily. One easy way to double-check this in advance may be through the candidate's LinkedIn recommendations section, if they have one. If you use a Boolean search to query it from inside Google while you're not logged in to LinkedIn, they will not know you have done so (as of this date July 5, 2015).

Bottom line: Interviews are artificial situations, at best. Like professional athletes, interviewees must be at their best for only a short period of time to win the interview game. The objective for the candidate is to get the offer. For you, however, it is to get the facts. Many people who sing in the shower believe they have talent, and inevitably some of those same people only discover the truth auditioning for shows like *America's Got Talent*. A little embarrassing, but no harm done. The same can't be said for your cost of hiring the wrong executive.

A PROGRESSIVE TWO-STAGE INTERVIEW PROCESS

Some worry a rigorous interview process (Figure 5.3) will somehow disengage a desired candidate, but we've found the reverse to be true. Fear not: A rigorous process matching the ideal candidate to the

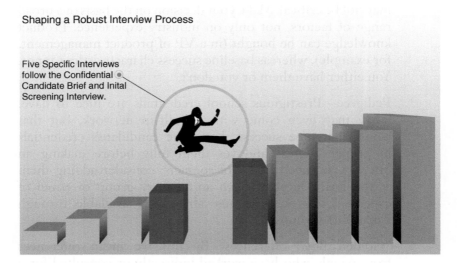

Figure 5.3   Hiring Greatness interview process.

ideal role serves everyone's best interests. Great hires are planned in a manner that provides your company a comprehensive platform to acquire and assess information on exceptional candidates, which helps map their leadership capabilities to your organization's culture and projected future requirements while maintaining the highest level of accuracy, quality, and confidentiality.

As previously mentioned, our success rate exceeds the industry norm by a substantial margin. We attribute part of our success to the intelligence our research staff gathers from industry clients and candidates through each executive search. We stand on the shoulders of giants, learning from everyone and everything we can. Since there are no formal educational requirements to become an ESP, nor diehard methodology guides to learn from, we've freely incorporated knowledge from a variety of disciplines including sales, marketing, psychology, and operations—not just human resources—into our executive recruitment processes. We're continuous learners out of both choice and necessity: Drawing from the experience of recognized leaders in the aforementioned fields keeps our success rate high and helps us stay ahead of trends.

The two-stage process we use is as follows:

- Stage I:
    - Benchmark interview
    - Initial contact
    - Screening interview and confidential candidate brief
- Stage II:
    - Face-to-face interview with two recruiters
    - Interview with the Search Chair
    - Interview with Search Chair and ultimate hiring authority (client)
    - Interview with peers and direct reports
    - Finalist candidate presentation and meeting with client

We're well aware that what follows describes a rigorous, formal approach to interviewing. But you'll find we advocate for a mix of formal and informal meetings with candidates who make the short list. Formal interviews lend themselves to canned responses, can be practiced, and may gloss over important social behavior. For these reasons we structure informal interview moments with hiring managers and during peer interviews.

Informal meetings, on the other hand, may favor candidates who are spontaneous or charismatic but not as thoughtful and may adversely influence your decision because they're likeable. Combining the two types of interviews and scripting behavioral and situational questions into discussions always yields more useful information, in our experience.

Yes, this is hard work. It's complex, which is why not everyone will follow it. Many will take shortcuts. But once you begin to interview this way the process begins to feel natural very quickly. And it's *so* worth it!

Beyond the Obvious: What We Look For

Executive interviews are different from those you'd perform at more junior levels, partially because there's more at stake in the outcome but also because well-crafted questions looking for predefined answers provide only part of the picture. Generally speaking, by the time a person becomes an executive, they've already proven they're highly proficient in answering traditional interview questions.

You hire greatness by first understanding who they are, their predominant leadership style, and their adaptability to adapt to your specific culture. Experience, knowledge, and track record are critical aspects of the selection process, but we can't stress enough the importance of evaluating the candidate's personal qualities. These are critical to ensure a cultural fit within your organization.

Outstanding Key Leadership Attributes to Watch For

All key leadership roles require individuals who can develop a plan, then assemble and lead a team to execute it. Our focus during the interview and evaluation process will be to find those select few candidates who are and have been successful within the framework of the client assignment.

Work Ethic, Enthusiasm, Drive, and Intensity

Leaders have a resiliency that pushes them to persevere, regardless of the task. The best leaders are adept at creating a deep level of trust with employees and stakeholders at all levels. They have a superior work ethic, extraordinary stamina, and the ability to create an energy-charged, enthusiastic work environment. Ultimately, they enjoy doing whatever it takes to get the job done.

Adaptability

At the executive level you're obviously looking for someone with a high level of raw intelligence balanced by well-developed emotional intelligence. In today's hyper-paced global environment you're also looking for those who can use their intellectual capacity to make quick, solid business decisions in tough competitive environments often without having all the details, so intuition is also important.

Passion

There comes a time in the process when the right candidate—your next great hire—develops a passion for the challenge and opportunity, and without prompting can articulate very quickly how they see their contribution making a difference. Watch closely to see how their perception of the opportunity evolves over the course of the interviews, because you'll pick up clues about what's important to them, which you can later use to close an offer and hire them.

Why Executive Interviews Are Different

Let's be clear: From the very first call, you're courting the candidate. It's essential in today's competitive recruiting environment that the candidate you "awaken" stays focused on your opportunity. It's not enough to find them and engage their idle interest. You need to make the position hugely attractive, addressing their "what's in it for me" (WIFM) curiosity with the opportunity. You need to closely couple your selling of the opportunity with an equally pragmatic approach to the underlying HR issues surrounding the position.

The Timing and Personal Characteristics Are Different

When interviewing someone for a key leadership role the interview takes longer than traditional interviews. It's a courtship process in the truest sense of the term, which requires you to pay attention to subtleties that reflect on the candidate's intent and authenticity. When we conduct an executive search, we spend a large amount of time getting to know the individuals as human beings, learning what drives them, and probing specific experiences and accomplishments. This allows us to find our preferred candidates who have a high level of honesty and integrity. It's imperative that the individual is a well-principled person: someone your people will trust and who shares values with the executive team.

The Energy Is Different

It is imperative that the candidate has the ability to create excitement as well as enthusiasm, and engage employees and stakeholders. To a great extent their ability to achieve ambitious goals hinges on their personal passion, energy, drive, and commitment around a shared vision. *This is the most difficult quality to evaluate in the interview process.* We're looking for candidates whose passion rises when they recount their successes, and who exude passion when telling the story. You can see a level of excitement and enthusiasm as they detail the who, what, where, when, why, and how of their accomplishments in the role. You can typically sense they're ready to do it again. We often hear this referred to as "fire in the belly," so watch for it and ensure it's genuine.

The Investigation Is More Intense

We focus on details when candidates talk about what they've accomplished: We probe to learn how things actually got done, because during the boom years in the 1990s many underwhelming executives were simply in the right place at the right time. If a candidate is unable to describe—in detail—significant technical events they were part of, they probably weren't the real architect but instead benefited from the "halo effect." As one of my favorite clients once remarked early in my career, "Even a blind squirrel finds an acorn now and again."

The Business Drivers Are Personal

We're also looking for candidates seeking a career progression with increasing levels of responsibility. Leaders are usually recognized early in their careers and are continually given more responsible positions. They rarely sit idle in their careers. How an executive advanced during the period 2000 to 2010 may tell a different story, and may expose a level of resiliency you'll appreciate—or a fatal flaw you can't live with.

Why You Always Conduct Face-to-Face Interviews in Pairs

When interviewing executive candidates you should do so in pairs. The risk of rejecting the correct person because of a personal bias is high. We all have biases and beliefs, even those we're not fully aware of, that may guide our decisions even if they have no bearing on a candidate's ability to perform the job. The average interviewer isn't trained to look past a candidate's veneer to examine the talent rather than the presentation, so the risk of passing on a viable candidate when interviewing alone is very high. Why risk it? Personal biases are another major reason we use the Confidential Candidate Brief (CCB) as our first real connection with potential candidates. The CCB is an impartial intermediary, blind to gender, age, race, sex, and other biases.

As a pair, one interviewer asks the majority of the questions while the other records responses, keeps the interview on track, and on time. The record-keeping interviewer is also responsible for posing follow-up questions if a candidate's answer isn't complete. Interviewing in this fashion facilitates an unbiased assessment of the candidate immediately after the fact.

FACE-TO-FACE INTERVIEW WITH TWO RECRUITERS

This is essentially the "candidate's story 2.0." The interview is longer and conducted by two ESPs at the same time.

Objective: compare the accomplishments, experience, and skills outlined in the candidate's CCB to the Position Profile and look for inconsistencies.

1. Assess communication skills.

2. Judge "fit" as per the Benchmark Interview.

3. Assess "executive presence."

4. Do a deep dive on leadership style and assess adaptability.

5. If interested at the interview's conclusion, confirm the candidate's interest in:

    i. Proceeding to the next interview with the Search Chair;

    ii. The role as currently as spec'd out, if offered; and

    iii. Any outstanding questions.

The First Hour

I always ask candidates if they have any questions for me before we begin. If they do, I answer them truthfully to the best of my abilities and defer the ones I cannot answer to a follow-up call after I get the answer(s) they're seeking. Then I begin with "I'd appreciate it—if you wouldn't mind—taking me through your career again like you already did, but allowing me to ask you questions this time along the way. So, take me back to when you were first getting out of college or university and roll through your career up to now."

The questions on my mind at this point are more focused on his or her contribution, leadership, adaptability, and personal style or "fit." I ask probing questions as the candidate tells his or her story and my recruiting partner takes notes. I'm looking to confirm the story and details they first told me during the recruiting and screening call. I ask a lot of follow-on questions like the ones below, and when we get to the most recent 10-year period in their career I dig deep for project specifics I can't find out about from looking at who they may have worked with on their LinkedIn profile.

In the CCB we asked two questions specifically, which I follow-up on as we go through their story again:

1. They were asked in the CCB, "What are your biggest accomplishments?" Most people answer relative to the role but I'm also interested in what they do outside of work. So if all their accomplishments are work-related, I'll query them about their "other" life as they take me on their journey of discovery. I want to understand how they establish goals and face adversity, because personal sacrifices can tell a lot about a person's character.

2. They were asked in the CCB, "What is the one thing you would change about the company if you could?" I can quickly peg a candidate's work personality if they immediately start listing their dislikes and the list is longer than a few, *and* if the list remains the same or very similar when they talk about other places they worked. At the very least you need to consider if the same conditions apply in the role you're recruiting for. Remember: Skills and experience are a given at this point. It's mostly about culture and "fit" now, and I'm looking for thoughtful answers and patterns of behavior at this time.

While this is our first face-to-face interview, the tone of our meeting needs to induce a normal business conversation. It's certainly not an interrogation and should never be construed as such. In this meeting we're seriously courting the candidate and, in turn, he or she is interested in the role as it relates to advancing his or her career.

As the candidate takes me along his or her career journey I press them for transparency. By asking these five questions, I get greater clarity:

1. How did you discover the job opening?

2. Why did you want the job?

3. What did you learn?

4. What did you accomplish?

5. Why did you leave?

The nuts and bolts of what you're looking for differs with every project, but in general here's what you should be listening to understand:

1. How did you find out about the job? Posted jobs are still where most people find out about new opportunities including: job boards, company websites, LinkedIn, and other social media sites, so that's certainly not a red flag. However, any candidate who's not being "found" for opportunities probably doesn't have the level of skill and experience that would have their accomplishments talked about by others as you should expect. Great leaders are talked about. The type of person you are after started early in his or her career to build a reputation for results that would naturally attract other opportunities without having to expend much effort. Some are the embodiment of living legends. Other leaders will have gone out of their way to draft them on to their teams. A consistent history of "being hunted" is what you look for.

2. Why did you want the job? Top performers can articulate why they wanted a particular job or took a lateral promotion. They have a plan and they're open to opportunities that advance it. The best are often given near-impossible tasks early and often in their career to hone their skills for advancement. Titles and money are secondary measures of success for these types of people. They know the kind of environment they'll excel in, but have also adapted well to new situations and continued to flourish. They understand what motivates and challenges them. Not only can they describe it, they actively seek it. They're likely to perform well in your role if the other factors all line up and the fit is good.

3. What did you learn in that role? Were they successful or did they fail? Do they accept blame for a failure or blame everyone but themselves? In either case, what were the lessons and how did they apply them in future situations? Does it translate directly to your requirements? If not, ask questions designed

to ascertain how this person learns. Even more importantly, ask if they're committed to a personal continuous learning program.

4. What did you accomplish and why was this important? This is a very telling question because the natural thing for most people is to take credit for saving the entire world single-handedly, without a team of some type. It's possible he or she did, and if so just move on to another accomplishment because you're trying to assess their innate leadership style and management skills. It's awfully difficult to build winning teams consistently unless you share the credit and encourage others. Narcissistic, command-and-control czars generally reveal themselves at this point in the process. These types are to be avoided at all costs—unless the role specifically calls for it, but few opportunities at healthy organizations do.

    a) You also want to determine if their accomplishments grew in size and complexity? How do they build their teams and alliances? What risks do they take? How high are the stakes? Highly matrixed organizations require well-developed persuasion skills to move even the smallest program forward. The more complicated the professional environment they're being recruited into, the more refined these skills have to be.

5. Why did you leave? Good people leave for better opportunities and more money. You're not looking for a saint, but people also leave because an employer is too demanding. Or the company has gone in a different direction. Or (the biggest reason) the employee doesn't get along with his or her boss or co-workers. When that's the case, don't be judgmental. Resist the temptation to ask for details. Pause for a long few seconds and give the candidate the opportunity to explain—if they choose to do so at that time. In the process, many candidates will describe issues with management or disagreements with other employees.

Follow-up on patterns that concern you. Some people don't ever take ownership and always see situations as someone else's problem. Even at the executive level, some people have consistently had problems with their bosses, which means they'll also likely have issues with the new boss if they're hired into the role.

The Second Hour

Interviewer Questions

At this point I have the candidate's CCB and résumé in front of me and I've already compared it to their LinkedIn Profile, if they have one. After the candidate goes through their story in detail again, and your interview partner has taken copious notes, it's your time to fill in some much-needed details that were probably glossed over but are critically important. Since I care more about the candidate's recent experience—roughly the last 10 years—I usually start with their current job and work backwards. That way I can dig deep into recent history and compress the discussion of older jobs if time runs short.

Next it's time to fact check for accuracy. I dig into their background for clarification wherever it's needed. I expect 100 percent consistency with the information on all fronts, but approximately 40 percent of the time there are small inconsistencies and 20 percent of the time there are large ones. If appropriate, I'll call them out by using a punctuated pause in the conversation. It quickly becomes obvious whether the candidate intended to be deceptive. Several times I've discovered seemingly unimportant stuff that has led to my ending any further discussions.

I always start my detailed fact checking by first covering the basics. This ensures the details don't come back and bite you, along with establishing some check points for the reference calls to come.

Next, in rapid succession I verify each former employer: start and end date, reporting hierarchy, team members, and accomplishments. If they've had many titles in one organization, I confirm them all and look to see if each new role was a promotion or advancement of some strategic nature. During this stage, I'm intensely probing for more information around things like:

Datelines—Some candidates choose not to detail their months of employment, only the years. You need to understand why: Is it because of an employment gap, or just a formatting choice? Ask for exact dates if they haven't been provided or were vague on the résumé they were asked to submit with their CCB (those instructions should be clear on the front page of the CCB). If they were between opportunities were they consulting, taking courses, or on the golf course? It makes a difference, as your candidate may have additional latent skills of real value.

Hierarchy—I ask the candidate to verbally sketch the company organization and where they fit, to whom they report, and their span of authority. I'm also interested in their peers and what they do. This gives me a clearer picture of the candidate's real responsibilities if it already wasn't clear enough.

Contribution—I always ask what shape the business was in when they joined. Were there problems? What were the top three short- and long-term objectives?

Authority—How many people were on your team? Did you make changes? Why? What was the outcome?

Performance —How did the business perform versus plan? Versus the past five years? What impact did you have? Why did your accomplishments matter to the business?

Behind the Scenes

Once the right candidate has been identified, has demonstrated a strong interest in the position, and you are considering taking them further in the process, one of the most critical stages of the search begins—the close. You need to confirm the candidate's interest and confirm the candidate will accept your position after every interview.

There are many things that can derail a search, but the single most frustrating is to find your selected candidate has become a reluctant bride at the end of the courtship. Make continuous feedback, which should be forthcoming from the Search Chair, a priority. Continue to seek the candidate's counsel at each juncture. Be quick to address all issues the candidate may have—no matter how trifling you may consider them—right up to the day the candidate actually starts.

THE SEARCH CHAIR INTERVIEW

This is the first interview the Search Chair will do following the benchmark interview. The Search Chair interview is done with the Search Chair and one ESP, generally the project lead.

Objective

- Assess communication skills and executive presence.

- Do a deep dive on their leadership style.

- Assess the candidate's adaptability.

- If you're still interested in the person as a candidate for the position at the interview's conclusion you must confirm the candidate's interest in:

  - Proceeding to the next interview with the ultimate hiring authority (in this case Fred), Search Chair, and ESP;

  - Accepting the role as it currently is spec'd out if offered; and

  - Any outstanding issues like relocation, financial handcuffs, spousal, and family special issues.

Yes, you need to sell throughout the entire interview process. But you need not do all the talking all the time— and if you do talk more than the candidate, you'll waste the opportunity to assess them against your needs. Instead, be cordial at every turn but strive to have the candidate do 80 percent of the talking. That 80/20 rule of their talking to your listening allows a skilled interviewer to understand the capabilities and shortcomings of the candidate and develop a purposeful, evidence-supported report.

The first meeting between the Search Chair and each candidate is designed to assess the candidate's suitability for the role, and his or her advancement in the interview process. By the time the Search Chair and candidate meet, the former will know a great deal about the candidate's background. Besides weekly updates from the ESP, the Search Chair will have received and reviewed the candidate's CCB, résumé, and interim reports from the candidate's previous face-to-face meeting with the two recruiters. The interim candidate assessment report should describe in detail how this candidate's background and experience match the needs described in the position profile. This meeting should last two to three hours with appropriate breaks.

After welcoming the candidate and thanking them for investing time to meet with the Search Chair, the ESP will confirm the candidate's interest and ask if they have any questions before the formal interview begins. The ESP will lead off the meeting by asking the candidate the same initial question asked when he first met with both ESPs, with a small significant change: "(Name of the candidate), can you spend ten to fifteen minutes now and take us through your career from when you're getting out of college or university and take me through your career—in 10 to 15 minutes." The time limit is shorter. We do this so that:

- The Search Chair can understand the candidate's background and progression beyond what may be detailed in the résumé and CCB;

- The ESP, who's listened to the candidate's story three times now, can check it for consistency; and

- It may also provide insight into the depth of interest the candidate has in the role. If he or she draws analogies from past experience or offers personal insights unprompted that's a good sign s/he's thought seriously about the role and can see accepting it if offered.

Following this discussion the Search Chair takes over from the ESP and dives in to the candidate's background with prepared questions, which initially focus on two primary areas of most concern at this juncture: the candidate's ability to deliver *the desired outcomes expected* from the role and their *interpersonal skills*.

To help assess the candidate's ability to deliver the desired outcomes, the Search Chair should drill down on one or two of the accomplishments the candidate detailed in the CCB. It's generally a good idea to ask for one or two business examples and one from their personal lives, because work-related accomplishments often require a team while non-business success is typically a solitary activity.

Listen carefully while the candidate speaks and don't interrupt except for clarification, if necessary. The ESP should take copious notes to compare with the Search Chair later. What can you glean from the language he or she uses to tell the story? Is he or she a team player, team leader, or both? Does he or she seem to gravitate toward one exclusively? Or is he or she a lone wolf? Compare that with how the department or organization he or she is about to lead functions—will his or her style work with your culture? Do the examples show that he or she has the ability to adapt to situations?

Now the Search Chair should ask for an example of where everything didn't go as planned. How does he or she explain it? Does he or she take responsibility, or does he or she try to shift blame on someone else? Is he or she quick to throw someone or another department under the bus? If he or she continuously revels in his or her own glory and blames others through his or her stories, you won't know to kick the ESP under the table until you ask him or her to take you through how he or she defines success.

To do this, simply ask these four questions and don't interrupt the candidate while he or she is speaking:

1. "How do you define success?" This tells you what he or she values and how he or she measures success.

2. "Do you believe that you have been successful?" That's a fairly general question, so it isn't unusual to receive back as "yes and no." That gives you an opportunity to drill down and get specifics.

3. "Did you succeed in achieving your performance objectives this year?"

4. "What specifically did you do?"

Successful people set specific goals. The acronym "SMART" is widely used and well-known, and the first letter, "S" stands for "specific."[11] Successful people make sure their goals are:

- Specific, clear, and understandable.

- Measurable, verifiable, and results-oriented.

- Attainable.

- Relevant to the mission.

- Time-bound with a schedule and milestones.

Next you want to ask similar questions that reveal insight into the candidate's leadership style, interpersonal skills, and goal setting for his or her organization. These three questions should be asked by the Search Chair at this point:

1. Flexibility/Adaptability—"According to Peter Senge, the one single thing a learning organization does well is to help people embrace change. Convince me/us that you are an effective

change agent by describing an experience or experiences from your past."

2. Interpersonal effectiveness—"Tell me about a specific time when staff reductions required restructuring of the workload. How did you do the restructuring? Who specifically did you involve? How did you involve them? Why did you involve those whom you did?"

3. Organizational stewardship—"Tell me specifically what you have done to create an atmosphere of trust and empowerment within your sphere of influence. What tangible results have you seen from your efforts?"

The last questions the Search Chair should ask before turning the conversation over to the candidate are about his or her personal goals.

That sequence of questions will take you two hours to get through in a meaningful way. The 45 minutes to next hour should be devoted to answering the candidate's questions. Following that, the Search Chair ends the session with two questions:

1. Why do you think you're a good fit for this opportunity?

2. What's your plan for making our organization better?

Note the candidate's reasoning and thought process. Write down his or her responses because you're going to want to compare them should the candidate meet the ultimate hiring authority. Throughout the meeting the ESP should take notes to later fact check.

Behind the Scenes

After each candidate is interviewed, the ESP and Search Chair share perceptions of how closely the candidate's experience fits the role and discuss at length the person's fit with the executive team. If either the ESP or the Search Chair has concerns or wants more background information on the candidate, this is noted for action by the ESP later. Using a specialized CRM program like Invenias, which is made specifically for the needs of ESPs and their clients, makes record-keeping painless.

If the candidate is going to be encouraged to continue in the process and meet the ultimate hiring authority, the ESP will begin informal referencing and fact checking. ZoomInfo can be useful in this regard because you can quickly discover who has worked with this candidate in the past. You can also use LinkedIn for the same purpose. Invenias is helpful at this point as well because it allows you to easily see who else you know who may know the candidate for potential pre-referencing. With Invenias you can start to build a reference list of people you want to talk to. Leveraging Invenias' search and import function will permit you to search LinkedIn and ZoomInfo.com if you have accounts. LinkedIn is also a good quick way to see who is related to whom, and how, for potential referencing purposes later.

Confirm the candidate's interest and pre-commit the candidate to accept the position again. Discuss compensation at length, including any golden handcuffs in effect. Finally, discuss counteroffers and understand what type of counteroffer they would accept from their current employer to stay.

THE ULTIMATE HIRING AUTHORITY'S INTERVIEW

Interview Time: 1.5 to 3 Hours

This is the first interview with the ultimate hiring authority, but it may include others depending on circumstances. This interview is done with the ultimate hiring authority, the Search Chair, and the lead ESP as scribe. The ESP may be asked to design the base interview questions. Naturally, the ultimate hiring authority will have received, read, and questioned wherever necessary all correspondence and reports provided by the ESP and Search Chair.

Objective:

- Validate the Search Chair and ESP assessment.

- Do a deep dive on the candidate's leadership style.

- Assess the candidate's fit and personal style—can I work with this individual? Do I like him or her?

- If you're still interested in the person as a candidate for the position at the interview's conclusion, the hiring executive must confirm the candidate's sincere interest in:

  a) Proceeding to the next interview with a group of his or her peers and the board, and

  b) Accepting the role as it currently is spec'd out if offered.

By the time a candidate first steps in front of the ultimate hiring authority, his or her skills, experience, and "fit" will have been systematically vetted by a trusted board member and two ESPs. The candidate was approached and invited to assess the opportunity because they're known to be the best of the best in their industry. They weren't looking for a job yet have endured a succession of multi-hour interviews. The Search Chair and ESP have documented why they believe that candidate is the right hire. But it's the hiring authority that has to work with them day-in and day-out.

It's a great convenience for the CEO to hand off the preliminary work of locating, identifying, and evaluating a new hire, but now it's time to step up and take responsibility for making the final call. He or she has to be willing to look the candidate(s) straight in the eye, ask some tough questions, and do a gut check before passing them through to the Search Committee.

Yes, I said gut check! I can hear the wailing and gnashing of teeth now from millions of well-meaning HR professionals—and they're 100 percent correct that "gut instinct" is unreliable and should never be used in an interview in the case of a young and uninitiated manager. But I encourage executives with 20 or more years of experience to listen to their guts. As Malcolm Gladwell points out in *Blink: The Power of Thinking without Thinking*, instinct is seldom wrong. A gut check is required.

Let me explain why following the rigorous process Mark and I outline can help you mitigate the risk of a bad hire:

- The functional spec meets the needs of the business plan.

- The candidates are already known to be outstanding. They are not looking for a new job nor are they between opportunities.

They've been systematically courted for months by professionals specifically for your role. At times, these candidates may be the result of years of cultivating a strong business relationship with these people on the part of the ESP.

- Your Search Chair is a board member and is on your side. He or she has the organization's best interests at the forefront. His or her reputation is seriously on the line and they will use every means possible to ensure the best executive recommendations.

- The executive search firm has skin in the game, and more than a passing interest in getting it right. Now is when it pays big dividends for your business-savvy HR exec to have convinced the executive search firm to warranty its recommended hire for one full year.

Speaking from experience, I can assure you that every ESP in the world understands how hard it is to do a search correctly the first time. No one wants to have to redo a search from scratch. Beyond the public humiliation, their time has been lost and there may also be a financial cost to them personally.

After reviewing the notes provided by the Search Chair and ESP, the ultimate hiring authority's focus during this initial meeting is to continue asking the hard questions to help determine the individual's fit with this team. Great executives are a lot like Super Bowl head coaches and are always measuring their bench strength against the other guy's team—and they're always looking for talent to shore up their weaknesses. Their job right now is to decide if the executive being presented can execute the playbook as part of that team.

At this juncture the search chair should lead the discussion toward the candidate's systems thinking and creative thinking abilities. The ESP should take notes while the ultimate hiring authority explores the candidate's thinking patterns, by asking probing questions such as:

Systems Thinking: 1. Tell me about a specific decision you made within your organization that had unexpected consequences outside of your organization. 2. How did you deal with those consequences?

Creative Thinking: 1. Explain the approach you use for performance improvement. 2. Explain specifically how you identify problems, what strategies you incorporate to measure the impact of the problems, how you deal with the problems, and how you measure success or failure. 3. Describe one such problem you dealt with from initial identification to resolution and closure.

Executives typically have healthy egos, but since today's successful work dynamic requires teamwork the traditional command-and-control structures don't work with today's knowledge workers. It is vital to gut check the candidate's innate leadership qualities, which include a review of their level of self-awareness, candor, flexibility, and genuine humility when leading a team. The Veterans Administration (VA) (of all places) provides a good example of how to steer the discussion in such a direction:

> Personal Mastery: 1. Everyone has made some poor decisions or has done something that just did not turn out right. Give an example of when this happened to you. 2. What did you learn? 3. What would you do differently?

How the candidate responds to this question will help uncover any narcissistic tendencies that would interfere with their ability to get the job done.

This meeting should last two to three hours with appropriate breaks. The meeting could lead to a private dinner with just the ultimate hiring authority and the candidate.

Behind the Scenes

This is a crucial meeting. By the time the candidate and the ultimate hiring authority meet, the latter will have received and reviewed the candidate's résumé, confidential candidate brief, and notes on all previous meetings with the Search Chair and ESP. At this stage the ESP may have lightly referenced the candidate as well. The ultimate hiring authority may also know people familiar with the candidate, and whether or not these individuals are approached for information needs to be discussed between the ultimate hiring authority, Search Chair and ESP. Confidentiality must be maintained or you run the risk of losing the candidate.

All compensation-related issues need to be confirmed before going forward. Discuss with the candidate the need for references, including who they would use and why should the job be offered to them. Don't leave the discussion of referencing any longer. If there are issues the candidate doesn't want you to know about, whom he or she chooses as references may bring them to light sooner rather than later.

THE SEARCH COMMITTEE INTERVIEW

This is the interview with the Search Committee, and is done without the ultimate hiring authority. The Search Chair and lead ESP are both present. The ESP may be asked to design the base interview questions for each of the Search Committee members and/or review all questions to be asked, mostly so there's no unnecessary duplication of questions. Naturally, the Search Committee members will have received, read, and questioned wherever necessary all correspondence and reports provided by the ESP and Search Chair. THEY DO NOT KNOW THE RESULTS OF THE ULTIMATE HIRING AUTHORITY'S INTERVIEW.

Interview Time: 3 to 4 hours

Objective:

   a)   Confirm the candidate's fit;

   b)   Select and close the candidate on the role.

   Note: This is not a perfunctory "meet and greet." It is make or break time.

The search is drawing to a successful conclusion. The ESP has culled a long list of more than 100 prospective candidates to a short list of 20. Through five successive interview stages the field has been pared down to two outstanding executives who the ultimate hiring authority feels would be excellent additions to the team. It's now the Search Committee's task to interview and help select the executive who can best accomplish what the organization's business plan expects from the role.

By this stage in the interview process the Search Committee members will have been fed a steady diet of impressions about all candidates after each successive interview, but they may not have heard any feedback from the ultimate hiring authority. If this is the case, the Search Chair should convene a meeting with the selection committee as a precursor to the final interviews with the short-list candidates. This meeting will provide the final opportunity for vetting the candidate.

Prior to the meeting, the Search Chair should courier a consolidated package of information to each Search Committee member's home that should include a) an itinerary for the meeting, b) the candidate's résumé, c) the CCB, and d) any anecdotal notes the Search Chair and ESP deem appropriate.

The best interview outcomes occur when the Search Committee receives advanced training from the ESP or chair on effective interview techniques. Training includes tactical coaching for each interviewer and developing ongoing feedback mechanisms that facilitate real-time sharing of insight and impressions with other Search Committee members throughout the process. The Search Chair should meet with the Search Committee to pose this question to the group:

- Given what we know about the candidate and what we need to achieve by staffing this role, what else do we want to discover about the candidate personally and professionally that we don't already know?

The answers to the foregoing question will then drive the executive search stakeholders, including the ESP, to draft a series of questions to complete the collective due diligence and prepare for the final Search Committee interview with the short-list candidates. Each Search Committee member will be assigned a question to ask the candidates while the other committee members take notes. This is a standard approach for the board and Search Committee interviews. The candidates will expect it and will come well prepared for the Search Committee interviews.

The most productive Search Committee interviews are structured, planned in advance, and executed with rigor. Typically, the Search Chair opens the meeting and introduces the candidate. The Search Committee has the full report on the candidate from the ESP through the Search Chair. They all meet the candidate and pose one of the relevant questions designed to complete the vetting process.

The objective is twofold: conduct a formal interview to find something the ESP, Search Chair, and ultimate hiring authority might have missed, and to also conduct an informal interview over lunch to expedite bonding and buy-in. The bonding aspect is a critical aspect of the close. Remember that the executive you're courting is about to divorce his current company and leave all his friends and relations behind. That's not an easy choice, and the decision is exponentially more difficult when there's a geographic relocation required. To vet and convincingly sell the candidate the two sides must bond. There must be a strong emotional connection that goes beyond the courtesy that's been extended by the Search Chair, one that extends to key players on the Search Committee as well.

Following the formal interview the Search Committee will adjourn to a luncheon with the candidate. It works best when the luncheon is off-site. If a candidate is going to let down his or her guard, he or she is going to do it in neutral territory. Remember to have dietary preferences as well as health and religious concerns prearranged beforehand with the candidate as well as members of the Search Committee.

Behind the Scenes

Following this meeting and while their impressions and thoughts are still fresh, the Search Chair and ESP should have a discussion ending in a go or no-go decision. At this point, further information shouldn't be needed. Following a good meeting, the ESP should be in a position to debrief the candidate later in the day and float a trial balloon offer. If there are still areas of concern then the ultimate hiring authority, Search Chair, and ESP should discuss the best way to handle it. Frankly, if this is the case at this point, the ESP has not been doing his or her full job.

THE CANDIDATE'S BUSINESS PRESENTATION

Throughout the interview process your focus has examined the critical elements of the job, the corporate environment, and the degree to which a candidate can respond to those elements. Essentially at each successive stage you've thoroughly assessed the candidate's:

- Set of demonstrated skills in relation to the tasks to be undertaken;

- Fit within the relationship structure of the organization; and

- Interest in undertaking the role they're being recruited for.

Interviews themselves, even highly sophisticated behavioral-based interviews, are still static. By this time I'm sure you're nearly 100 percent convinced which candidate is the right one, but you've still never actually seen them in action. This is why we highly recommend you have them prepare and deliver a formal presentation to the Search Committee. Donald Trump utilized such formal presentations on NBC Television's *The Apprentice*.

High-level presentations are a normal part of most sales and marketing executives' weekly tasks. We'd ask the short-list candidates to prepare a twenty-minute presentation for a fictitious new account. For non-sales and marketing executives, and especially for change agents, consider asking them to lay out their 30-to-60-to-90 Day Plan and present it to the Search Committee, Search Chair, and the ESP.

The presentation is important but is not a test. There are no right answers. What you want to assess is how they use their time up to the day of the presentation. You'll get a fairly accurate snapshot of their work habits and leadership style, and the chair should observe how they approach preparing for the presentation. Did they ask for the correct amount of help/guidance in preparing the presentation? Are they lone wolves or armchair generals? Is that an asset or a liability in the role you're staffing? The exercise will give you insight as to how they:

- Think

- Strategize

- Organize

- Present

- Handle pressure

- Think on their feet

- Communicate

Watch closely and take notes. You're not looking for perfection, but are they:

- Prepared?

- Convincing?

- Credible?

- Logical?

- Compelling?

Now compare notes with your colleagues.

- Does everyone "feel" the same about the candidate?

- Are the reasons for their selection or disqualification appropriate?

- What further questions need to be asked?

- Do the candidate's future goals, their skills, and the role *you need* filled all align with the company's requirements?

- Most importantly, based on their preparation and delivery of the presentation, do you now believe they are sincerely interested in your opportunity?

Listen to Your Gut

Don't be afraid to consider how you feel about the candidate. I know, "Feelings are neither scientific nor logical." But this isn't the USS Enterprise and you're not Mr. Spock, so do a gut check before making the final decision. The accuracy of the gut check is enhanced by asking out loud and reflecting on these five questions:

1. Do you trust this person? Trust is binary—there is no gray. Answer yes or no and proceed (or not) from there.

2. Have they made you a believer in their candidacy?

3. Do you honestly believe your company would be better off if they were to come aboard?

4. Are any of the concerns raised about the candidate critical to the job in your organization?

5. Do you sense a deal can be made which is generally in line with the compensation levels of the rest of your team?

A negative answer to question number one is a showstopper. A negative answer to question number four requires that you have another interview, dig into their answers to your questions, and settle it. Don't expect to be able to cover every issue without exception. Just be certain you understand in detail the job and environment in relation to the skills, background, and personal qualities of the final candidate. Doing so will put the odds of success in your favor.

NOTES

1. Personally, I subscribe to J. Paul Getty's interpretation of Matthew 5:5: *The meek shall inherit the Earth, but not its mineral rights.*
2. https://hbr.org/2007/07/the-making-of-an-expert.
3. www.execunet.com/e_features_article.cfm?contid=3170&welcome=5344.
4. www.execunet.com/template_network_print_friendly.cfm?id=3254& popuptype=mediacontent.
5. Simon Sinek, "Start with Why: How Great Leaders Inspire Everyone to Take Action," *Portfolio*, 2009.
6. Ron Wiens, "Building Organizations That Leap Tall Buildings in a Single Bound," *Ron Wiens*, 2012.
7. www.mhs.com/Default.aspx.
8. www.wired.com/2015/04/hire-like-google/.
9. http://mavweb.mnsu.edu/howard/Schmidt%20and%20Hunter% 201998%20Validity%20and%20Utility%20Psychological% 20Bulletin.pdf.
10. www.wired.com/2015/04/hire-like-google/.
11. http://hr.fas.harvard.edu/files/fas-hr/files/fy14_fas_guide_to_goal_ setting_9.23.13_v2.pdf.

CHAPTER 6

Due Diligence
Don't Hire a Liar

Everything yields to diligence.

—Antiphanes

P rior to arranging the face-to-face interviews, I sent Carl several interim reports for his review and general information. He and Fred had previously vetted the Position Profile and Confidential Candidate Brief. As the primary ESP, my job was to keep the Search Chair in the loop and explain how and why each of the proposed candidates fit the criteria. If I had any concerns I also highlighted those issues. Prior to Carl meeting any of the potential candidates for the first time, each of them would already have spent three to five hours with my team—including face-to-face meetings with Michael and me—and a supplemental cross-referencing phone interview with Mark.

Carl and I flew back to Milwaukee. We were set for the second stage of face-to-face interviews with the short-list candidates Michael and I had selected following our marathon visit a week earlier. As the primary ESP on the project, I wanted to combine the benchmark interview and Search Chair interview in one meeting. I was comfortable each of the five candidates we were bringing forward could do the job and were each interested in the opportunity.

Each candidate easily met our well-defined criteria but in this case, as always, the wild card was their fit. All five candidates were so very different, personality-wise, and were each about to be questioned by a sharp and enlightened mind by anyone's standards. I was looking forward to it. As Search Chair, Carl was acting on Fred's behalf and leading the Search Committee but I'd never seen him in action. I know I'd embarrass Carl by calling him a sage but, based on my observations throughout the past six years, that's the uncanny scope of his judgment. Highly principled and of impeccable integrity, I've found Carl Albert to be fierce, fair, wise, and direct in all our dealings. One learns very quickly that venture capitalist, industrialist, philanthropist, and humanitarian are incomplete monikers to describe the full scope of Carl's humble strength of character and depth of business acumen. So you can understand why I was looking forward to getting to know Carl better.

Every time I do a search it's critical I get to know the Search Chair. It's a must. I need to understand how they process and interpret information, along with how they assess, treat, and value people. I also need to understand what fit they're looking for in the executive candidate, along with how skillfully they can interview a potential candidate.

Another must is to understand the Search Chair's bias and manage it, so the correct person is hired for business reasons rather than sentiment. Our goal is to attract someone based on the key performance indicators needed for the company to achieve its business plan. There's no room for any type of prejudice or alma mater favoritism. Impartiality is important. I've found that people educated in the disciplines of law, medicine, finance, and engineering—in that order—make the best Search Chairs. They tend to be clear thinkers swayed by logic and little else.

Carl's background in law was interesting to me, but it was his business savvy that most intrigued me and I was looking forward to our debriefs after each interview. I knew my summation skills would be put to the test. But I wasn't prepared for the virtual teardown following our first interview.

Carl and I had both arrived in Milwaukee on a sunny mid-afternoon under a bright blue sky. It was a short ride to our hotel, the same one Michael and I used the previous week. I was impressed when the doorman remembered my name because we'd only stayed a few days the previous week, and I hadn't gotten into enough trouble to be memorable.

We were supposed to meet our first candidate at 4 p.m. However, no sooner had I arrived than he called and asked to push the meeting out to dinner instead, saying he would make the arrangements. A few hours later we were being seated in an upscale steakhouse down the road from our hotel. Dinner was interesting. The candidate was relaxed and regaled us with a colorful but concise trip through his career. And then it was over. Carl suggested we walk back to our hotel and talk along the way. I agreed and as soon as our feet touched the sidewalk I turned and asked him what he thought. He deferred, saying, "He's obviously well qualified. His experience and education fit well. How do you think he'd get on with Fred?" Now, you know a good lawyer never asks a question to which he doesn't already know the answer.

I was up. Forget about me assessing his skills—he was now assessing mine. So as we turned to point our feet toward the hotel I said, "I don't think he would, and here's why...."

As I was explaining my rationale for *not* taking this candidate forward to meet Fred, I was carefully watching Carl's expression trying to tell if he agreed, pausing occasionally to ask him to confirm my thinking. As we deconstructed our dinner meeting, assessed each other's observations, and slowly walked home I was comforted to know we were both on the same page for the same reasons. Interviewing is as much art as it is science. The science is in the regimented approach to sourcing and engaging desirable candidates in a dialogue. The art is the harder part. Getting "to the door" is relatively easy; getting "in the door" is quite another. It takes years of practice to finesse the dynamic situation of convincing a senior executive to take on a new opportunity.

I told Carl candidate number one was indeed qualified to do the job but during dinner displayed both poor listening and judgment skills, as well as a total disregard for anyone but himself. For example, despite several subtle hints and one not-so-subtle hint, candidate number one regaled us with his exploits throughout the entire evening. Now, most job search coaches will agree you have to sell yourself in an interview. They are correct. But humility and balance are important too. By the time candidate number one was sitting across from Carl and me, he had already spent five hours with the primary gatekeeper—me. I had already been sold on his experience and skills. We would not have been here otherwise. This was the candidate's opportunity to demonstrate his soft skills, do a deep dive into areas of the company not discussed in the position profile, and understand the expectations of the board. He didn't do that.

Before crashing for the night I called Mark Haluska back at the office and debriefed him. Mark needed to be familiar with what new filters to apply as he continued recruiting and qualifying prospects. (*Note:* Out of habit (and professional paranoia), most ESPs will continue to run a search until the Friday after the selected candidate takes their post.)

The other glaring issue, which I hadn't picked up on during our first three conversations, was his heavy focus on the word "I." The word "team" was certainly never referenced that evening. As we pressed for details around his accomplishments it was obvious they couldn't have been done without assistance. Suffice to say candidate number one's lack of emotional intelligence was counter to Tulip's culture. This was good news, because we had just experienced a bold display of what wouldn't work "fit-wise" and I was confident that over the next few days one of the remaining four candidates would be a fit.

On the way home, Carl took me on a side trip to a Milwaukee favorite: Kopp's Frozen Custard. I had no idea anything this heavenly delicious existed on earth. It was ambrosia for mortals, I'm sure. I was now a disciple of the frozen custard cult! This really helped make the five-mile walk more palatable—and oxymoronic—for me. Carl is trim and lean and in great shape, and I'm not. So I think our daily walks to Kopp's were by design. At the end of the week I felt like I'd lost 10 pounds!

The next morning we had a great interview. Candidate number two had the polar opposite personality to number one. Day three and day four of interviews went well, too.

And then, on the afternoon of the fourth day, we met with Jim. Despite being retired, Jim continued to sit on several boards of directors in the area and was very active in the business community. Jim showed up neatly dressed in a dark blue suit, as had the other candidates, but with no tie. Like me he had "wrestler's neck," and probably had to have his shirts custom made. He came dressed to be comfortable. No pretense in this guy. He was affable and pleasant like the last time we'd met, but it was clear Jim wasn't here to just sell himself—he wanted to learn more about the company. He thanked Carl for making himself available and then we went straight to business, just as he had with Michael and me the week before. I appreciated the consistency.

Although not from the plastics manufacturing industry himself, it was clear he'd done his homework. He was quick to relate his experience to the organization's needs and articulate where he saw opportunities to add value.

Michael, however, had a slightly different impression of Jim than I had formed. He was hesitant about Jim because he appeared slow and plodding, whereas I viewed him as thoughtful and engaged because at every point of contact Jim drilled down into the organization, its business practices, and the industry trends. It was a great meeting about the business.

Later that evening, Carl and I wrapped up the week's meetings with a summary assessment report I produced for Fred's review. We made arrangements for Fred to meet the remaining short-list candidates with us at the plant in Milwaukee, then headed out for that rewarding 10-mile round trip walk to Kopp's.

At Tulip's facility in Milwaukee, Carl took over my role and led the interviews while Fred probed specific areas he was most interested in with each candidate. I acted as scribe again, noting details I'd need shortly for reference checking purposes. Of the three people that we invited to move forward, two interviewed extremely well. One disqualified himself early in the interview with a TKO caused by a discrepancy in his "personal story." Remember, by the time I bring candidates in front of the ultimate hiring authority, I've heard their story three times and have already started to fact check their background. If a candidate suddenly veers off-script when questioned on a specific aspect of their experience, the red flag goes up.

At the end of the day Fred was torn between two superb candidates—the ideal scenario for a recruiter. In the end Fred decided Jim Rulseh was more seasoned and a better fit with himself, Carl, and the board.

Upon my asking, Jim produced a reference list 22 people deep containing everyone I wanted to speak with (I was taking notes about who he worked with at the time) and then some. References were all the appropriate direct supervisors, peers, and subordinates going back nearly 30 years. We contacted everyone and cross-referenced the information to get as true a 360-degree picture of Jim as possible.

We still had to conduct some remaining due diligence, but for the most part, Fred's hunt for his next COO and successor was over. It had, however, been a needlessly long search. If the firms he'd originally hired had just been forthcoming with their hands-off restrictions, Fred could have instead hired a boutique search firm to accelerate a comprehensive search from the appropriately large pool of talent and without a doubt, the position would have been filled two years earlier. But it made little difference now. Fred had found his professional soulmate, after all, and his name was Jim.

And in our view as ESPs with decades of experience, it was a match made in heaven.

CATCH ME IF YOU CAN

In Steven Spielberg's film *Catch Me If You Can*, Leonardo diCaprio portrays Frank W. Abagnale, a master impostor and forger. Abagnale worked all over the world using false identities as a doctor, lawyer, college professor and as a co-pilot for a major airline company—all before reaching his twenty-first birthday. This is a very funny and entertaining movie, which begs the question: "How did this guy ever get hired?"

It seems it's not that hard. Con artists, masters of deception, and people right in your town fool the system daily, robbing the economy and putting people's lives at risk. According to the American Management Association and the U.S. Department of Justice:

- Employee theft and dishonesty costs U.S. businesses between $60 and $120 billion per year (not including the billions spent on protecting against theft: guards, security systems, etc.).

- $36 billion in annual workplace violence.

- The average employee embezzles $125,000 over the course of their career!

And that's the average person, so imagine what an organized guy like Frank could do. These statistics underscore a serious problem—the incredibly expensive price and high stakes consequences of hiring the wrong person into your organization.

Over the past 30 years I've interviewed more than 60,000 people. Even for seasoned ESPs like Mark and me, it takes a lot of work and preparation to see past the veneer of most jobseekers. It's very difficult to get candidates to open up and be themselves. Due in most part to the candidate-centric books on how to interview, most candidates "dress for success" and come prepared to dazzle the interviewer, to "close the deal," or to "take the relationship to the next level," so to speak.

The high-tech sector in particular morphed the hiring process into one-sided sales pitches, where interviews and reference checks were a formality and rarely done for fear of losing a hot candidate. "Time-to-hire" became the mantra of the day. For a few years it seemed every candidate had an agent or personal spin-doctor, and the results were predictable.

In the real world, the only way to get an accurate assessment of a candidate is a thorough interview process and to talk with their (most likely past, but if possible current) co-workers, who are the people who know the jobseeker's job performance best. This brings us to our subject today: reference checking.

Poor morale, high turnover, lagging sales and the old "disappearing market share" trick are all symptoms of a bad hire, one that could have been prevented had you known all along about the candidate what you found out later. And if that's not bad enough, there's always the cost to jettison the excess baggage. Firing isn't cheap. An entire industry called outplacement evolved because firing extracts such a heavy toll on those who have to do it. Then, of course, there's the endless litigation and the whole negligent hiring aspect of improper hiring. But the correct reference checking process can help you avoid all that pain, and a little foresight and proper planning can help keep you out of trouble.

So why don't people simply check references all the time? The first reason is that it's quite tedious, and by the time most managers get to the end of a hiring process and find their star candidate they just want it to be over. Most employers also don't like giving references because of the fear of litigation from an unhappy, unemployed former colleague whom they simply told the truth about, so they assume there's little point. After all, what candidate would actually give you a bad reference? It can be quite frustrating. (Not to contradict what we just said about candidates providing bad references, but *on rare occasions* it does happen.)

Here are some of the other reasons clients don't bother checking references. Perhaps you've heard them as well:

- "References only give you name, rank, and serial number;"

- "It's very difficult to get honest answers from a reference;"

- "No one gives negative references for fear of litigation;" and

- "Who would give you a reference that would say something negative?"

If this sounds like you or your organization, I have good news—you don't have to be a "reference check refugee" anymore.

There are a lot of people who don't like giving references. These people will go out of their way to avoid you. Fortunately life doesn't have to be that way all the time, and we're going to show you how to warm up even the most frigid reference so you can glean all the information you need to make an informed hiring decision. We're going to tell you exactly what to say and how to say it, so people will gladly answer your questions when you're looking for your next Jim.

Why References Are Critical in the Hiring Process

References remain the only real means to assess who's got the skills to take your company where you want to go. They represent your opportunity to separate fact from fiction, and the sincere candidate from the professional interviewee.

This guide has been produced to level the playing field and teach you, the employer, how to properly reference check to help ensure you actually hire the person you want.

References are the key to guaranteeing quality hiring—but only if done correctly. Résumés and interviews, the other two major hiring variables, are unreliable by themselves. Referencing is the glue that binds the process. Résumés aren't reliable because they can be intentionally misleading, and interviews are a crapshoot for most people. If those last two statements sound worrisome or even shocking to you, you're not alone. So let me elaborate on those points for a moment.

Why Résumés Are Unreliable by Themselves

The recent proliferation of résumé factories, coupled with higher levels of unemployment, have led to a situation that some of us call "credential creep." Credential creep is the fine art of exaggerating. Sometimes it even means out-and-out lying on a résumé on the off-chance an employer won't or can't reference check to verify the details. But the fact is, people do lie and exaggerate on paper when they're looking for a job. In a tight economy—heck, even in a booming one—the slightest edge is often what makes the difference between securing an interview or being filed away in the circular cabinet.

Credential creep can range from a candidate claiming they had greater responsibilities than they actually did, to claiming they worked for a company when in fact they didn't. To illustrate that fact, let me tell you about the experience of one of my clients:

> A few years back, Brian, one of my clients in the United Kingdom, called me shortly before Christmas. He was preparing to hire a fabulous candidate he'd met at a party and wanted my input on the offer. On paper the fellow was a dream come true: a sales vice-president with 20 years' experience from three of the world's largest systems integrators. Pedigrees like that are rare. The nice chap had even provided written references from the presidents of these firms. They were sterling—a little too good, actually. I insisted on checking the references myself and because I'd worked with him for more than 10 years and had hired more than 20 of his key staffers, he agreed. It turned out that "Reginald"—or "Reggie," as he referred to himself—had a deep and rich fantasy life. Yup, he'd made it all up. Everything. None of the presidents had even heard of him. Beautiful forgeries. When confronted with the lie, more lies were told. Something about being undercover with MI-5. Needless to say, we didn't hire him.

This may be an extreme case but nevertheless people do fudge, embellish, augment, and incorrectly describe their credentials. Take, for example, the former president of Lotus, Mr. Jeff Papows, who got in trouble several years back for misunderstandings surrounding his education and military service record. According to the *Wall Street Journal* as reported through *The Register* (www.theregister.co.uk/content/archive/4047.html), Papows is:

> "Not an orphan, his parents are alive and well. He wasn't a Marine Corps captain, he was a lieutenant. He didn't save a buddy by throwing a live grenade out of a trench. He didn't burst an eardrum when ejecting from a Phantom F4, which didn't crash, not killing his co-pilot. He's not a tae kwon do black belt, and he doesn't have a PhD from Pepperdine University."

Granted, these are unusual cases you aren't likely to run into. But résumé creep happens at all levels, and with great frequency.

Heather Bussing, California employment attorney and legal editor of the *HR Examiner*, says, "Most résumés have the basic information right. The rest is a matter of interpretation. Candidates often claim qualifications or experience that they don't really have in order to get the interview. They think if they can just meet the hiring manager, they will 'wow' them; they can learn the rest when they get there. This not only wastes everyone's time, it damages the candidate's credibility. Even if the person is hired, lies on résumés can be used to justify firing the employee down the line, even if they were fired for something else."

And an article in *Maxim* magazine titled "How to Lie on Your Résumé" actually does exactly what the headline promises, harnessing the guidance of Jim Petersen, author of *How to Lie on Your Résumé—and Get the Great Job You Want!* (Ariza Research Press, 1998):

> Some résumé cheats create false references that are difficult to check. Jim Petersen, the Cleveland-based publisher and author of *How to Lie on Your Résumé—and Get the Great Job You Want!* found a way to do this when a computer company he worked for went belly up. "About a half dozen of us stood around the parking lot and agreed to act as supervisors to give references for each other," he recalls. Petersen always gave a fellow conspirator a ring before a recruiter was going to call, to make sure they had their story straight.

As you can see, a little effort is all that's required.

Why Interviewing by Itself Is Unreliable

There are innumerable books and success coaches nowadays to help coach or train a candidate in how to perform during an interview, which means most jobseekers are more skilled at interviewing than the interviewers themselves. Interviewing is now just as much an outright gamble as it is a tool in the hiring process, and the odds are stacked in favor of the jobseeker.

For most hiring managers who occasionally interview, the process is a farce. It reminds me of a gentlemen's tennis match with everyone dressed in white and careful to remain immaculate. Questions are asked and answered: back and forth, forth and back, with very little in-depth discussion. The mood is light and congenial, nothing like real life.

Reading this book and following our process gives you two benefits when reference checking:

1. The interview process is rigorous and focused on finding facts; and

2. If you take notes during the interview of the names of the people, places, and projects the candidate mentions, you can easily follow up later.

Interviews rarely reflect real-life situations or real-life people. For this reason alone you need to reference people thoroughly. We North Americans live in a world where gregarious extroverts often win out over the quiet, steady performers you should be hiring. As they say, "bullshit baffles brains"—and it's far too often true, I'm afraid.

Reference checking is often the last and, indeed, sometimes the only way to separate who's really got the skills and who's just a fast talker. Frequently interviewers extend offers based on their first impression, gut feel, or chemistry with little regard for the hard evidence that proves which candidate is the right one for the job. If this isn't enough to convince you of the necessity to reference check every candidate, then let's talk about your legal obligations.

Negligent Hiring

Can you be held liable if you don't check references? *You bet.* As a matter of fact, as if it isn't tough enough just to make a profit these days, many companies have been held liable for crimes committed by their staff. These crimes have ranged from murder, to rape, to theft—and the liability was all made possible in the United States because of negligent hiring lawsuits. Negligent hiring varies from state to state, but essentially means a company can be held liable for failing to conduct an adequate pre-employment investigation into a jobseeker's background. If an employee has a history of misconduct indicating a propensity for criminal behavior, which an employer could have discovered through a background investigation, the employer could be held liable for any resulting injuries. Failing to adequately investigate before hiring can expose the employer (your company) to liability for actual injuries, pain, suffering—and even punitive damages. You can be putting your whole firm at risk.

"Employers can be liable to their own employees and everyone that employee encounters at work for discrimination, harassment, and dishonest conduct. Employers can even be liable for employee violence if they knew or should have known the person had a history of similar conduct," says Heather Bussing, California employment attorney and legal editor of the *HR Examiner*.

Negligent Referral

Can you be held liable if you give a false reference or bury the truth? Yes. In a widely publicized example of a negative referral case, a lawsuit was brought against Allstate Insurance Co. that was settled before going to trial. But a Florida judge ruled that Allstate could be sued for punitive damages for concealing the violent nature of a former employee who killed co-workers at Fireman's Fund Insurance Co.:

> In this case, the wrongdoing allegedly occurred when Allstate wrote a recommendation letter saying the employee was let go as part of a corporate restructuring. In truth, he had been fired for toting a gun at work. Fireman's Fund Insurance Co. said it relied on the letter from Allstate when they hired him. In January of 1993 this man shot five Fireman's Fund co-workers in the company's cafeteria. He killed three of them, before fatally shooting himself. One of the survivors and the families of those who were killed filed the suit against Allstate. One positive outcome from the tragedy was the resolve and subsequent legislation to ensure this didn't happen again.

This is of course another extreme example, but is one more good reason for doing references.

In the United States, 35 states have passed laws that protect employers by granting them immunity from civil liability for truthful, good faith references. While the laws vary by state, the statutes specify that an employer will be "presumed to be acting in good faith unless the current or former employee can prove that the reference provided was knowingly false, deliberately misleading, malicious, or in violation of civil rights laws."

As a professional recruiter with more than 1,000 successful projects under my belt, I assure you most employers want to follow the Golden Rule: "Do for others as you would like them to do for you." Many employers will answer your reference questions, and provide more than salary verification and dates of employment, if you ask the right way.

Bottom Line

There are two main reasons you need to check references:

First: You have to make sure the star candidate you're about to hire really can do the job. References can help to substantiate or nullify the facts and impressions you have gathered from your interviews; and

Second: You need to protect your employees, customers, and yourself from a negligent hiring suit.

To reference effectively you need to do much more than casually call the people on your candidate's list of references. Personally, I always find the composition of a candidate's reference list fascinating. When it's full of people who can't directly talk about his daily work, I know immediately there's a problem. I likely have a candidate who's trying to hide something. So whom should you call?

PROFILE OF A GOOD REFERENCE

The most important aspect of any reference check is not the questions—it's choosing whom to ask. Yes, whom you contact is actually more important than the questions you ask. You can, in fact, have the most rigorous reference check form known to mankind, but it won't help one bit if you ask the wrong people.

How to Determine Who to Talk To

You likely already know that most candidates stack the deck in their favor when asked for references, but this bears repeating: Unless you specify with exactly whom you want to speak, their list may be filled with people ready to sing their praises. And can you blame them? If you really, *really*, *REALLY* wanted a plum role like the one you've been recruiting for, wouldn't you do the same thing? Okay—maybe you wouldn't, but many people would. Many candidates don't want to risk having someone tell the truth, but this can't stop you from getting at that truth.

So where can you obtain the most objective information? Like most people you probably realize a person's past job performance is a good predictor of their future performance. The theory is that a star will perform well regardless, and for the most part, this is true. If the candidate did a great job at "ABC Company" chances are he or she will do a good job for you.

So who can tell you the truth about the candidate? It's not his or her priest, best friend, or drinking buddy. It's probably not his or her spouse, either. Rather, you need to talk to the people who can judge the candidate's ability to do the job for which they're being recruited. The best references are people who have *recent*, first-hand experience with the candidate on the job. Most often, direct supervisors, peers, and subordinates are best placed to have observed the candidate's performance in the level of detail we require. Typically, these will have to be former supervisors, peers, and so on.

Back in the interview chapter, we told you one of the main reasons for interviewing in pairs is so that one of you can scribe notes (of course, both of you are taking mental notes as well). Remember when you asked about their accomplishments during the interviews? You noted the names the candidate mentioned who were also involved and you should have been fact checking, unobtrusively through LinkedIn and other means, as you were going.

The purpose of the reference check is to obtain comments and observations about the candidate's performance and experience related to the job. It's of little value to obtain a reference's opinion, unless you're very confident in their judgment. And if you don't know the reference personally, which is most often the case, you have limited opportunity to clarify their credentials or capacity to make sound judgments. To assist in this, I suggest you always make sure you ask about and thoroughly understand the professional relationship between the candidate and reference.

Relatives and Other Useless References

Don't use personal references. Relatives and friends are of very limited if any value to you as a reference. Their opinions can't possibly add any insight into the candidate's work habits on the job. His buddies don't know what he's like to work with. Character references have their place, but it's not here.

The Human Resources Department

The most frustrating and, I would contend, irrelevant references are those from the human resources department of the company where the candidate last worked or currently works. Why? Two reasons: because they don't work with the candidate on a daily basis so they can only comment with second-hand knowledge or anecdotal information. They won't be familiar with the candidate's day-to-day performance, either, unless he or she is a superstar or a complete dud. Most HR departments are also hesitant to reveal anything, no matter how true, which might lead to legal action. If they choose to comment, it's usually just to tell you that "Yes, he or she worked here." That isn't what we're looking for. And, by the way, if the candidate is actually a superstar or a dud, they may try to intentionally mislead you anyhow.

Useful References

The best references to check fall into two major categories: direct and indirect.

Direct

The most useful references come from people who are, or have been, professionally involved with the candidate's day-to-day work: past supervisors, peers, and subordinates. Make sure you clearly understand each of the relationships between the candidate and his or her references before you begin. Obviously the reference questions you'll ask his or her former CEO aren't the same as those you should ask a former peer or subordinate.

360-Degree Feedback

Bear in mind, no one person will be able to give you all the information you'll need to make an informed decision. You need to check the candidate's references slightly differently, from boss to peers to subordinates, to get a complete picture of his or her competencies. Each reference offers another perspective, and another piece of the puzzle.

- The candidate's direct boss assigns responsibilities.

- The candidate's peers know what an overachiever the person is.

- Most importantly, the people who work directly for this person—the candidate's former subordinates—know everything the candidate's former boss and former peers don't.

- For better or worse, a candidate's clients (such as a sales executive would have) may be able to tell you things about that person that people back at his office would have no knowledge of.

This type of 360-degree feedback is enlightening, to say the least. And frankly, next to this person's boss, the candidate's subordinates will provide the most insight into his character.

Here's what you do when the candidate hands you his list of references. First, determine if the people on the list are who you need to speak with, then ask the candidate the following questions to assess the suitability of each reference:

Questions to ask a supervisor about a reference:

1. Did/do you report directly to him or her? For what length of time? (Less than one year is too short a period to form a valid impression).

2. Did/do you complete or contribute to his or her performance appraisals? How many?

Question to ask a peer about a reference:

1. Did/do you work directly with the candidate as part of a team? For what length of time? (Longer is better).

Note: If you clarify the relationship at the start with the candidate and find the reference unsuitable, simply explain the situation and ask for a more suitable reference. However, most candidates aren't used to this degree of rigor when they get to the end of the interview process. We'll explain exactly how to set this up during the interview stage so it isn't a problem.

Referencing Supervisors

The best possible information on how life will be with the candidate will come from the candidate's boss—who should be the ultimate hiring authority at his or her current or former employer. Generally speaking, your peer at the candidate's place of employment is more likely to be truthful with you if you call them directly rather than someone else doing it for you. After all, you're in a better position than anyone else to drill down on specific concerns you may have, or to query them on the finer points of the candidate's role.

We always insist that clients check at least one reference personally—always with their counterpart—and double-check two or three others. Often that even means having the client call and redo references we've already done. As well, the candidate's former boss's boss may provide a different perspective on how he or she performed.

We'll talk about this in greater length later, but in the meantime remember that even if you don't do any other references personally, you as the hiring manager **must** do the reference on the candidate with your counterpart at the candidate's old firm. There are no exceptions to this rule.

Peers

The qualities most in-demand today are the ones the candidate's peers are probably in the best position to comment on—leadership skills, communication skills, a bias toward action, and passion. We typically do at least two peer references for every supervisory one. The same ratio applies with subordinates. A candidate's peers can give you a true picture of his or her strengths and weaknesses as they pertain to his or her job function and how he or she supports that executive's business unit. We even ask them to rate the candidate against his or her peers and the former people who have held that position, just in case there's someone better I should be recruiting.

Subordinates

No one understands better whether the candidate is pulling his or her weight than his/her direct subordinates. Failed projects, blown budgets, poor management skills can all be fixed by a hard-working team stranded below a poor manager. Subordinates also know where all the "dead bodies" are buried … you know, those projects that were never quite completed properly, or the one that cost the company a million dollars to fix. Likewise, it might be good to know that a few dedicated subordinates followed the candidate over from his last gig and are likely to do it again when he or she moves.

Clients (When Appropriate)

Talking with your candidate's clients can be most interesting. Clients know what this person is like when not in the office. They can tell you if this person makes promises that he or she (or the company) could not possibly keep, just to close a deal. They can tell you how he or she handles conflict resolution over a product or service when there has been a problem. They'll tell you if your candidate is a good ambassador for their current employer, and so on.

Indirect References

Did you know you're not limited to only checking the names the candidate gives you? Well, you're not! It takes a bit more work on your part at the front end of the interview process, but it's often not what you know, but whom you know that makes the difference in getting a clear picture of a candidate. The stakes are high but always worth the time, effort, and expense (think insurance instead) to go beyond a candidate's prepackaged list.

In many cases, unless you've done some advance work we'll talk about later, you're better off not taking the references given by the candidate. You can often find excellent reference sources through your industry and professional associations. By doing a little of your own research, you may tap more objective sources with less or no coaching from the candidate—not that the candidate would do that, of course.

The higher the candidate's visibility in the industry, the easier this is to finesse. Indirect references can be a treasure trove of insightful information. If your industry insiders know the candidate by reputation only, you'd better find out if it's a good reputation or not. Often, contacts at firms that are direct or indirect competitors of the candidate's firm can provide useful information.

You can even keyword search Google to uncover nuggets of information. If you can, try this on LinkedIn, too. And remember to make certain you put the candidate's name in brackets, and realize that there are a lot of "Bob Smiths" in the world, so don't automatically assume you've found information on your Bob Smith without deeply scanning your results.

Before talking to any reference, inform the candidate of your intentions and have them sign a waiver, which allows you to verify information and absolves you of any legal actions resulting from your research. Ask your human resources department to have the waiver drafted by your corporate lawyer in compliance with your local state or provincial labor legislation. Don't attempt to do this yourself because litigation is costly and it might cost you your own job. We'll talk more about the specific how-to tactics and questions to ask later in the chapter.

Referencing Is a "Do It Yourself" Project

We're often asked who should check references and, simply put, it's a DIY project. This is the one job that shouldn't be delegated. If the candidate is going to report directly to you, you need to do the reference checking personally. No matter how thoroughly you prepare someone else, you are in the best position to drill down on answers that appear vague or off the mark. You understand the intricacies of the job, so you'll be able to think of additional questions that won't occur to others. All in all, it's in your best interest to get the facts directly.

If you don't have the time to do a thorough job yourself, and feel compelled to assign the task, then compromise by assigning just part of the reference checking to your most trusted assistant, but reference check the candidate's former boss yourself.

As a general rule it's not a good tactical move to call the candidate's current boss unless the candidate has expressly indicated permission. As I said before, your counterpart at the candidate's present firm is likely to be more open to speaking with the ultimate hiring authority personally than some third party who's simply going through the motions. CEOs should speak to CEOs, presidents should speak to presidents, managers to managers, and so on. The camaraderie afforded by your respective positions will prompt a more honest response. Be prepared for real candor because the higher up you go in the company hierarchy, the more candid the responses.

THE MAIN EVENT

The Complete Reference Check Process

If you're like most people, you may not appreciate the specific steps you should take before and during the interview process to make reference checking an easier and more successful exercise. To most people references are what you do AFTER you decide whom you want to hire, but an integrated interview and reference process is your best bet against a dishonest candidate.

SETTING THE STAGE

Prior to the interview decide what's important in the job. Have the Position Profile right in front of you. This sounds so simple, doesn't it? If only common sense were a touch more common. Alas, I can't tell you how many times a client has backed away from hiring a candidate because they were hung up on factors that had nothing whatsoever to do with the job—like an aggressive personality in a salesperson when in fact that's just what the job required, or the number of times HR insisted on hiring a team player when what the CEO really needed was a kick-butt, take-no-prisoners Attila the Hun—because she or he needs revenue from the new product line yesterday!

Clarify Your Hiring Objective

You must understand clearly what you're looking for before you interview even your first candidate. You of course already have the job description, Position Profile, and the candidate's CCB. If you haven't already done so, list in order of importance the top six functional tasks to be performed, the desired personality type, and direct experience the position requires. Use these to decide what you need/want, along with knowledge from references to validate your assessment of each candidate. Working from our database of 400 reference questions, we handcraft a reference guide for every search we perform. Our questions reflect the KPIs of the role, related accomplishments the candidate revealed, and the impressions and unresolved concerns (if any) noted by anyone involved in the interview process.

For example, if systems thinking is an issue, make sure you focus on it during the interview. Jot down whom they worked with and what they accomplished so you can verify the candidate's story later. Most companies don't take note of the specific details, and later on find it nearly impossible to verify the details of the candidate's accomplishments. That's often a fatal mistake. You don't want to put yourself in a situation where you have to call the candidate back later and say, "Your reference doesn't remember ..." or "Who can verify?" At best, you look incompetent. At worst, your hard-won candidate might think you're questioning their honesty and turn down your magnificent opportunity.

An excellent way of reinforcing to a candidate that references will indeed be checked is to start the interview by casually remarking, "Ms. candidate, obviously we're very interested in speaking with you about this opportunity. If you become interested in accepting the role we'll check your references and, by the way, we want you to feel free to check us out, too." You can also tell the candidate that you won't make them a job offer without unfettered access to their references. The result is that most candidates are likely to stick to the facts during the interview, and will later provide you references that will talk to you.

Throughout the interview ask one or two key questions you intend to ask their references. Jot down their responses—the "who, what, when, where, and why" of their accomplishments. Drill down on their accomplishments to get real specifics. For example, if they "increased efficiency by 100 percent," ascertain if they did it alone or as part of a team. This is an especially useful exercise. Later you will compare answers with references, and if there's a difference between what the reference says and what the candidate said you'll be in a position to clarify.

Figure 6.1   Several of the areas of information, which a good reference check will capture.

Conducting the Reference Check on Your Ideal Candidate

After weeks of intense interviews you've concluded that candidate X is the one. His or her experience, attitude, and skills are exactly what you want. He or she is your ideal candidate. Now it's time to get down to business and find out if your candidate is the real deal. What are your options for reference checking the candidate (Figure 6.1)?

Here's what you should be thinking about.

What was the nature of the reference's relationship to the candidate? Was it business, personal, or both? If they worked together, was there a reporting relationship? Was the reference a superior, peer, or a subordinate? If there was no direct reporting relationship, in what capacity did they work together? What was the nature of their last contact? When was it?

What was the reference's title and responsibilities at the time the two worked together? What is the reference's current title and responsibilities? (This helps establish the reference's credibility.) For example, if the reference was previously the corporate controller and is currently the president of the company, the reference's comments should be weighted appropriately. This also helps us view their comments in the proper context.

Ask the reference to describe the business, revenues, number of employees, lines of business, and anything else about the business that may be an important measure of the candidate's accomplishments.

For example, for a sales manager one such parameter might be the amount of sales growth (expressed in both dollars and as a percentage) and whether this growth could be attributed to a price increase, or real growth in the number of units sold.

If the reference is a former subordinate, what kind of a boss was the candidate? Ask him or her to comment on the candidate's skills as a manager, interpersonal skills, and skills as a motivator in terms of fairness, consistency, willingness to defend, promote, and/or mentor his or her people, keep promises, and develop staff.

Ask the reference to comment on strengths and weaknesses, keeping in mind the candidate's relationship with the reference. This is an important question, which should consistently be asked, regardless of the candidate.

Dead Trees

Be wary of all letters of reference provided directly by a candidate. Pre-written references can be very misleading. Many are written at the time of termination. Firing a person is a very sensitive task and there is a tendency on the employer's part to be full of praise with few, if any, negatives. Experts will tell you that candidates may even have written such letters themselves.

Several years ago I was suspicious of some so-called reference letters a candidate provided from his overseas employers. At the time I remember being concerned over the resolution of the photocopies: They were quite hazy. (So was he, frankly.) I actually sneaked a peak at the file this candidate left on my desk, only to find the "originals" he'd been down the hall photocopying for me contained signature blocks cut and pasted onto corporate letterhead. He'd simply written his own letter and pasted the president's signature in the appropriate place. Quite ingenious—*not*!

I don't know if this fellow was betting that I wouldn't call his former employer in the United Kingdom or that, if I did, the chairman of this multibillion-dollar company wouldn't take my call. In any event, he bet wrong. I did a full background check on him, and it turned out he truly was a thief and a liar. Needless to say, Interpol was informed of his whereabouts. You just can't make this stuff up!

The Hard Way

Writing to companies to request a reference is usually ineffective. It takes too long and there's little or no degree of candor. Too often, your letters won't be answered even after multiple follow-up calls.

Face-to-Face

An in-person visit isn't always practical, but when you're hiring an executive it's worth the effort. They're often difficult to set up, but will produce the most candid responses and give you the opportunity to detect nuances—raised eyebrows, limited eye contact, dubious expression, or hearty belly laugh. References are also far less likely to lie straight to your face, especially given the recent legislation around negligent hiring. Face-to-face references are very effective if you have any nagging doubts about a candidate. And if all else fails, you can Skype.

The Best Way

The telephone is a wonderful tool. Phones are fast, inexpensive, and nearly everyone has one—or two. I guess you can tell I use the telephone 90 percent of the time. As far as I'm concerned, if you're well organized and focused, it's the best tool. It's been my experience that references are far less guarded over the phone than when you see them in person. The telephone also allows you to ask spontaneous follow-up questions, and if you listen closely and pay attention to the tone of the reference's voice you can often detect enthusiasm (or a lack thereof).

TACTICS TO ENHANCE YOUR REFERENCE CHECKING

References don't need to like you, but it sure helps. Here are a couple of suggestions to facilitate loosening the tongues of even the dourest matron.

If possible, try to find out something about the reference ahead of time. Use Google to query their latest speech or corporate news release. You may have a few things in common—the same hobby, the same sports interest, the same area of residence, same school, or, better yet, same business contacts. The best way to find out this information is to ask the candidate, during the interview, to tell you something about each reference. It can be a great ice breaker when you call. If you can't find any personal information, then chat about the weather or current news before you begin. Most importantly, assure them from the outset that the entire conversation will be kept in strict confidence and none of their feedback will be revealed to the candidate.

Keep the discussion conversational. If a reference senses an interrogation is in the offing, they'll tighten up and not share as much as they might have otherwise. Speak with a smile in your voice to encourage references to be candid with you. It's wise to be friendly when you speak with them— friendly, but not familiar. The stories the reference tells are as important as the tone of voice used to tell them. The calmer the reference, the more information you can gather.

Ease Them into Your Process

You must respect a reference's time. Planning is important. If you ramble on, the reference will cut the conversation short long before you get the information you need. It's important to know which general questions you'll ask all the candidates' references, and also determine which specific questions will help clarify any concerns you have with each of the candidates.

It also helps if you can give the reference a brief overview of the basic functions of the job you're trying to fill. This makes it easier for the reference to compare your job to the one the candidate held with them. Call ahead to schedule the reference call, and send them the Position Profile to review as a reference. When you're ready to begin talking with references, establish rapport first. Describe your role and your potential interest in the candidate.

The questions you ask a reference should be virtually identical to the questions you'd ask the candidates themselves. Indicate that an important reason for your inquiry is to obtain guidance on how to supervise the person most effectively. A future focus and a little flattery will go a long way toward getting a reference to speak freely.

You'll get more effective responses to your probing questions if you start with simple ones. The first few sample questions below are easy to answer—just facts, so there's no pressure on the reference. You'll notice the reference is also not challenged to give their opinion. After briefly introducing yourself, begin with these basic questions.

Qualifying Questions

For Supervisors

- "Did/does the candidate report directly to you? For what length of time?" (Less than one year is too short a period to form a valid impression. If that's the case, find someone else.)

- "Did you complete or contribute to his or her performance appraisals? How many did you do?"

Peer or Subordinate

- "Did/do you work directly with the candidate as part of a team? For what length of time?" (Longer is better.)

Are their answers consistent with the candidate's? Are they qualified to act as a reference and comment on the candidate for this role? If you determine they are indeed a good reference, then follow with these warm-up questions before launching into your full reference check:

- "I'd like to verify the dates of employment, from _____ to _____."

- "What was his/her function (title)?"

- "How long did he/her work for you?"

- "Were his or her earnings $_____ per _____?"

- "Did that include bonus? Overtime? Incentives?"

- "Who did he or she work for prior to joining your company?" Always ask this question just in case your candidate had a short stint somewhere else he or she neglected to tell you about. You need to know, because there may be other things that slipped his or her mind.

These are simple questions. They're supposed to be. Many hiring managers don't even ask the basic questions we've already asked, but we're just getting started. These questions will help put your reference at ease and establish a congenial tone from the start. In fact, because the reference is likely to have given references for other people they may rest easy on the assumption you're finished, it doesn't hurt to lull them into a relaxed state before bringing out your "big guns."

Basic Subjective Questions

Next, get the reference openly talking by asking how long and in what capacity they've known the candidate. Now you're ready to lead into more complex, subjective questions requiring their opinion.

- "What were the candidate's strengths on the job?"

- "Were there areas in which he or she should improve?"

- "Was he or she dependable, a team player?"

- "How would you compare his or her work with others who held the same job?"

Cross-Referenced Interview Questions

Ask them about specific projects the candidate discussed, and compare the reference's answers with those the candidate gave during the interview for consistency. For example:

- "What was this person's biggest accomplishment at ABC Corp. in your opinion?"

- "What do you anticipate I will find to be this person's real strengths, and what areas would benefit from constructive coaching or mentoring?"

- "This position interacts with X types of coworkers or customers in Y types of situations. How does that compare to what this person did for you, and how well do you think he or she will handle these interactions for me?"

Don't be afraid to ask pointed questions regarding your areas of concern. You want to know about the very areas you're testing for in the interview process: flexibility, interpersonal effectiveness, organizational stewardship. You'll also want to know about his or her adaptability to the corporate structure, general pleasantness to be around, potential for leadership, and suitability for periodic promotion. If applicable, ask about the candidate's relationship with vendors, customers, and professional colleagues.

Some of the most awkward questions may prove to be the most useful. It's not fun to ask these questions, but you need to know—so ask!

- "Why did the candidate leave your company?"

- "Are they eligible for re-employment?"

How to Evaluate References Effectively

Discover the Real Reason for Leaving

You need to discover the real reason a candidate left each of their previous jobs. Not just because you're afraid of a negligent hiring suit, but because the candidate may have a negative employment pattern of which you need to be aware. This can range from violent behavior, as in Allstate's case, to simply self-promoting their abilities beyond their real competencies.

Getting the answer to this question is almost always difficult, because the word "fired" is rarely used. It's often couched in different terms such as, "We agreed to disagree," or, "We mutually agreed to part ways," or, "He was reallocated to a more suitable department."

You need to understand the circumstances behind each move. Was the candidate moving up? Is he or she always being moved around? You need to know the truth before you make a decision, especially if the candidate was not forthcoming with the information during the interview process.

Here are a couple of reasons I have been given by references more than once for an employee's leaving that are pure hogwash, along with the quick retorts that may prompt them to fess-up.

Reference says: "He (or she) wanted more money."

You say: "Why didn't you think he (or she) was worth it?"

Reference says: "She (or he) did such a good job she (or he) effectively made his job unnecessary."

You say: "You mean you couldn't employ such a great executive elsewhere within the company?"

Be Realistic and Objective

Neither longevity on the job, promotions, or raises are necessarily proof that an employee was much more than adequate—and remember, most people are average. Sometimes incompetent people who were very well liked have been known not only to survive on the job, but also to advance. At some organizations it's a "last man standing" situation. This is more often true in the public sector than the private sector, and very often the case in family businesses.

Carefully question the validity of comments made by former employers, especially negative information. It's not uncommon for employers to let negative feelings show through when an employee resigned for a better position, especially if it's a salesperson or key engineer who went to a competitor. People have long memories.

Likewise, employees terminated for poor performance may have worked out a deal with former employers to ensure a positive reference. So you can see why the peer and subordinate references may be critical for an accurate assessment.

It's Good to Be Paranoid

Don't overlook the obvious telltale signs. If a candidate can't come up with several contactable references—if all their former employers have "gone out of business," or every former supervisor is "no longer with the company"—you've got a problem. Don't hire the person. Those are clear indications of danger. At the very least, thorough reference checking will become mission impossible.

Be ruthless. You've just run the candidate through a rigorous interview process on purpose, so as to not make a mistake. Surprise! You and the candidate are still talking. So you need not be overly anxious to hire, yet you need to keep the momentum going. Complete your homework, always, in every way! Reference checks are the surest way to secure your company's future—to keep out the cons and attract the leaders who have the talent you want.

The end result is that, after talking to the references, you should have information on:

- The candidate's significant accomplishments.

- The depth of others' feelings, positive or negative, about the candidate.

- What management guidance or further professional development is required.

- Leadership and personal style.

- Relationships—internal and external.

- Depth of technical and professional skills.

- Career progression and career interests.

- Reasons for changing jobs.

- Problem solving skills.

- Predominant leadership style.

- Strengths and weaknesses.

Behind the Scenes

Hiring greatness requires an aggressive pursuit of the very best—the top people whose skills mean the difference between victory or vanquished. This requires real detective work, the willingness to encounter dead ends, solid research skills, and the persistence to unearth the information you need to find about your candidates.

With the reference data at hand, does everything indicate that the candidate will fit into the job and your company? Think through the information you've collected. Use it in conjunction with your interview impressions. Read between the lines. Consider what the people you've talked to are really saying, and take action accordingly. In his book *The Art of the Steal*, Frank W. Abagnale tells the remarkable story of how he parlayed his knowledge of cons and scams into a successful career as a consultant on preventing financial foul play—that is, after he got out of prison.

This story had a happy ending for Frank. Make sure your story does too, for your sake, your organization's future, and your employees.

CHAPTER 7

Sealing the Deal
The Future Is in Your Hands

Take time to deliberate, but when the time for action has arrived, stop thinking and go in.

—Napoleon Bonaparte

T he week before flying to Los Angeles for the Search Committee interview had been very busy. Asking a candidate for their references is always a tipping point: How a candidate reacts when you ask for references is very telling. By the time I actually ask, I've already spent better than 20 hours with them. I know their life story and career history in detail. I know their accomplishments and a few of their failures: who they worked with, and who they moved on from. Heck, at this point I can probably predict what they had for breakfast that day. That's because I listen intensely every time they tell their story, and take copious notes when they're deep in conversations with members of the Search Committee.

When I ask someone for their references, I'm hoping they give me the names of people I've already heard of from all that listening. And I wasn't disappointed by Jim. No one was missing from the list I'd already compiled privately. I was sure he had nothing to hide and was genuine, that his "what you see is what you get" swagger was authentic and that my 1,000th search would come to a successful conclusion. Well, let's just say I wasn't disappointed: Jim had listened carefully to what I said I needed, and that's exactly what he provided. Jim's list contained the names, phone numbers, and email addresses of 22 people with his relationship to each clearly spelled out. Most of them were names I recognized from his "war stories," although a few I did not.

I called them all. Thank goodness I'd taken shorthand in high school, because I spent another 20-plus hours fact-checking before we wrote our recommendation to hire and filed the references for Fred, Carl, and the Search Committee to review. Going into this final meeting I was cautiously optimistic. Everything had gone as it should during the search, which was essentially over. But Jim still hadn't met the family yet, and we all know how important that is during a successful courtship (in fact, he hadn't yet met some members of the board—which included Fred's sons). So as I drove to the hotel to pick Jim up I reviewed my plans for the afternoon, recognizing that the whole search could blow up in the case of a bad impression on either side.

Jim was in a good mood as we drove through the mid-afternoon traffic. But then again, Jim was always in a good mood. I'd noticed this early on, and it was something several of his references had commented on during the reference checks, so I knew it wasn't an act. We talked about family and business. It was clear Jim had been reflecting on Tulip's industry position and foreign competition. He shared some ideas with me that he wanted to bounce off Fred as the day went forward, which reminded me of the first time Michael and I had met him. Unlike all the other candidates, Jim hadn't come intending to impress us. Instead, he'd been on a fact-finding mission. I could tell back then he already knew the answers to the questions he was asking, and I sensed he again was prepared to assess the situation, dig deep, and get at the truth. There was no question he was prepared to walk should the Search Committee offer a tepid response to his line of questioning. I don't know what prompted the comment from Jim that he'd bought my book *Guerrilla Marketing for Job Hunters* and had read it twice, but I laughed. His enthusiasm and sincerity were encouraging.

Arriving at Tulip's offices, we were welcomed by Fred and Carl and shown to the same boardroom with the solid mahogany table in which we'd originally met months earlier. One by one, the remaining members of the Search Committee and Fred's sons met with Jim. Taking up my position as observer and scribe, the afternoon passed quickly. Soon enough Jim, Carl, Fred, and I were huddled in Fred's office where Fred made a formal offer to Jim. Jim accepted. And that was that, or so I thought.

What happened next, though, is permanently etched in my memory.

Following the successful conclusion of our negotiations (everything had been settled days in advance), Fred announced we were all going to dinner to celebrate. A few hours later, Jim and I stepped into a stateroom at Fred's country club where Fred, in true old world style, had arranged a reception befitting a visiting dignitary (I'll refrain from making any wedding reception-related comments here). Fred, obviously pleased and proud of what he and the Search Committee had accomplished, proudly introduced Jim to his lovely wife and extended family, as well as the other invited guests. It was classy and, at the same time, a shrewd businesses move to welcome Jim to the Tulip family this way. Plus, our meal was elaborately scrumptious.

That evening was a fitting conclusion to Fred's search, and I was impressed but not surprised as Fred took the reins. Fred had been a savvy client throughout the entire project. He'd been forthright in his expectations, transparent in all discussions, and authentic and responsive whenever Carl or I needed anything. He had great expectations from the outset and because of this was, as we say in the business, "he was all in."

FIVE RULES TO DEVELOPING A WINNING OFFER

Okay, you're sold. You've been out to dinner with your ideal candidate and his or her significant other. Your Search Committee and its chair have given you a resounding thumbs-up. References are complete. The requisite background check was completed by HR. Your industrial psychologist confirmed it's a great fit. Now's the time to develop and negotiate an offer, right? Well, no, not really. ...

In fact, the time to begin the offer process was back during the very first interview. By subtly approaching the offer stage early on, critical stumbling blocks or even deal-killing issues are identified and dealt with well before a formal offer is made.

If you hired an ESP, then by the time the Search Chair first met the candidate all parties were also aware of the candidate's compensation expectations. Behind the scenes the ESP will have been shaping an acceptable offer by floating trial balloons back and forth between candidate(s) and client. Where cash requirements are an absolute, allowances can then be made and adjustments considered long before the actual offer is made.

Successful offers account for the needs of the individual as well as those of the company. When one-sided deals are struck that favor either the company or the candidate, the relationship is often short-lived and

may be counted in seconds before one party turns and bolts. The resid-
ual effect of a win-lose proposition is a relationship that never happens.

To develop and negotiate winning offers, follow these basic rules:

- Understand the candidate's primary motivation for wanting to join your company and sell to it, especially if you know you can't meet all the cash requirements. In some cases psychic cash is worth more than cold hard cash.

- Structure the package to reinforce the position's KPIs as defined in the job description and highlighted in the position profile. Candidates expect to be assessed against firm performance metrics. In short, don't present them as a moving target.

- Make sure the candidate fully understands all features of your company's compensation program. We sometimes find that a company has a better benefits program than most hiring executives or candidates realize. Conversely, at times we've also found the company's first offering wasn't as attractive as they initially believed.

- Ensure the offer is competitive with the outside market and equitable internally.

- Be creative as needed. Such things as signing bonuses and extra stock options can push a candidate in your favor, while not creating undue disruption within your organization.

Talk about your expectations throughout the interview cycle, then listen. Be particularly sensitive to comments like: "My wife/husband will not relocate"; "We have a child in high school"; "My non-compete hasn't expired"; "I have a large bonus that won't be paid for six months"; "My stock options are only partially vested." These are red flags that should be explored immediately to determine their true impact.

Also watch for comments like: "We're a two-income family," or, "My daughter has two horses," or "I will need to buy a new car." These are not deal stoppers. They are bargaining chips. The candidate is setting the table for the coming negotiations.

You'd be surprised at what we've done:

- Orchestrated the relocation of a horse.

- Placed a CEO's spouse into a new job.

- Arranged storage for a collection of 1,500 bottles of wine.

- Purchased a classic cherry-colored 1966 Gibson ES-335 electric hollow-body guitar—all in the interest of closing the deal.

I must confess the costs to my clients in all cases were less than the costs associated with bridging the candidate's insurance policy between employers—but, more importantly, it went a long way in proving to the candidate that we were listening and really did care about his or her needs.

It's actually a good sign if the candidate is already calculating how to do a deal if the interviews conclude favorably, and as mentioned your ESP should be doing this on an ongoing basis during the interview process. A professional ESP will provide you with this type of discovery.

The Five Elements of Compensation

Once the groundwork has been done to define the issues and decision points in a candidate's mind, and your company's compensation parameters are understood, a compensation package can be developed. In every executive compensation package there are five basic elements to consider (see Figure 7.1).

Within these five basic elements there are countless variables, of course. But to help structure your thinking on the way a compensation program should be developed, the following are the major elements to consider.

Elements to Consider

1. The candidate's current compensation package (your ESP will have acquired this during the recruiting, interview, and debriefing sessions from the candidate);

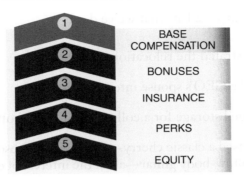

Figure 7.1 Five elements of compensation.

2. Market rates for comparable positions (because you know the candidate will have researched this thoroughly on Glassdoor .com or other such websites);

3. Rates of pay for peer level executives in your company;

4. Your company's compensation policies;

5. Some other factors that may influence the candidate's decision:

    • Future professional growth opportunities; degree of risk in your company; future reward potential such as bonuses or equity appreciation; amount of dislocation in the candidate's life; the candidate's need for the job and strength of interest in joining your company; the amount of risk you're taking in hiring that candidate; and so on.

    • Idiosyncratic candidate "wants" or "desires" that defy logic or objectivity and could be deal breakers. Examples I've encountered in past searches included periodic round-trip flights to visit a child at college, and a gas card for jet fuel (the candidate owned two planes that he used for continental flights).

PRESENTING THE OFFER

The Executive Search Professional (ESP) is there to help negotiate terms of an agreement satisfactory to both parties. They'll have been consciously doing this ever since the first phone call with the candidate many months ago. They also need to ensure your second choice is also kept enthusiastic, in case you're unable to come to terms with your first choice. The more delicate issues regarding compensation negotiation should be handled by your ESP well in advance of your final meetings—especially if you're expecting issues around base salary and/or power sharing within the defined role.

Making a major life decision like this may be very difficult for the candidate, particularly if it requires relocation. Several times during the offer stage the candidate may even get cold feet and renege. Unfortunately, it's often easier for a candidate to simply make a non-decision and stay put. In this situation, it's critical the ESP and Search Chair continue keeping the candidate focused on the opportunity at hand by focusing on the candidate's WIFM (the "What's In it For Me" factors we discussed in previous chapters).

When the final offer is made you obviously want it to be accepted, and there should be no surprises if the ESP has verbally delivered your offer. Any details that needed to be negotiated or clarified will have been dealt with. The offer is good to go pending final reference checks, which can usually be completed within five to 10 days, during which time your Search Chair and ESP will be in constant contact.

THE BEST CANDIDATES HAVE THE SHORTEST SHELF LIVES

On occasion over the years, the authors have had the pleasure of working with companies that really understand how to finesse a deal. We'd like to showcase one for you now.

We'd just finished a rather complicated search for a company in Chicago, Great Lakes Dredge and Dock, whose CEO Jonathan Berger has flair (to put it mildly). To help close one particular executive vice-president search, following the last meeting Jonathan couriered a package to the executive's home. Included with the offer letter was a high-gloss copy of the company's annual report (see Figure 7.2) featuring a forward-thinking "thank you" for the candidate's contribution, as well as a dozen long-stemmed red roses for his wife. This creative and personal touch drove home to the candidate how

Figure 7.2 Great Lakes Dredge & Dock offer letter package.
Special thanks to Jonathan Berger and Bailey Rubin at Great Lakes Dredge & Dock Company, LLC.

much the company valued him. So when the search is completed, don't be shy about celebrating appropriately with the candidate and Search Committee—it might just be what seals the deal in the candidate's mind.

HOW TO EXTEND THE HONEYMOON PERIOD INDEFINITELY

Tulip's search for a chief operating officer concluded successfully. By following our process, we expect your search will conclude successfully as well. But that's not where the story—or your placement—ends. Hiring and on-boarding a new executive is one thing, but keeping him or her becomes your next challenge because competition for the best and brightest will only continue intensifying.

After all the effort and expense an organization goes through to acquire and develop top talent, how do you ensure your new executive stays—that they don't get raided or head for greener pastures? The first 100 days is typically the bellwether. To get off to a solid start, we follow up with both parties and schedule set times for the Search Chair to touch base with both the candidate and ultimate hiring authority to ensure objectives and promises are being met. We also send both parties a copy of George Bradt's book, *The New Leader's 100-Day Action Plan: How to Take Charge, Build Your Team, and Get Immediate Results.* When you combine the candidate's 30-60-90-Day Plan presentation with George's book, you have the basis for a fast start on the right track.

Through the years and talking with executive A-Players on a near-daily basis, our combined 45-plus years of executive search experience has taught us what executive talent retention is really all about. Year in and year out, the very same issues always come to the forefront. We use these issues to initiate the dialogue that will eventually lead to plucking them out of one company, and into our client's. We methodically comb through and use issues we know have been the catalyst for engaging executives in conversation long enough to listen to our offers. None of these tactics should come as a surprise, because we've written about this over the years in several HR magazines.[1]

There are ten keys to keeping your prized executive. They're all derived from three fundamental management principles covered during the recruiting and interview process: challenge, communication, and compensation.

Challenge

A stimulating and challenging environment provides the first three keys for executive talent retention.

1. Vision and Goal Setting—At the Top

Your key executives want to know where they fit into the big picture and how they can position themself and plan for their own success. Your job is to help them see it. How? Communicate the company's goals, its vision, and its mission. Put performance goals in place, with a formal review process as part of the program to measure performance at realistic intervals. When executives' personal goals are tied to the company's own mission and goals, they feel connected and can gauge their own value contribution. This makes it very difficult to woo them with the promise of "greater challenges."

2. Expectations

High-energy, high-impact executives like to run with the business equivalents of a Peyton Manning or Michael Jordan. Healthy egos thrive in an environment that not only recognizes excellence, but expects it. There's tremendous pride that goes with being associated with the best and being recognized as a top performer. So make your company a magnet for exceptional employees. Earn a reputation for top-level performance by expecting executive excellence. Others will want to join you, and your current staff won't want to leave.

3. Creative License

A challenging work environment offers not only the ego-satisfying contentment of reaching tough goals, but also the spirit-building, competition-crunching exhilaration of finding new ways to reach them. Sadly, the opportunity for creativity often disappears the week after a new hire starts. This is when the company is most vulnerable to losing him or her to a counteroffer from their former employer, or a shrewd competitor. Don't let your new executive think they're now just a cog in the "system."

> *"A soldier will fight long and hard for a bit of colored ribbon."*
>
> — Napoleon

Communication

This is the management tool that allows vision, expectation of excellence, and creativity to become second nature to your company's success. Good communication offers four more keys to executive talent retention.

4. Dialogue, With Attitude

Everyone's talking about communication, and there's a dizzying array of courses that stress communication via Quality Circles, TQM, empowerment, and team building. Most have failed to live up to their promises, as will most of those that replace them. Successful programs are based on an attitude allowing two-way dialogue to exist and flourish. The best performers will go where they can be heard. Make sure they don't need to travel further than the ultimate hiring authority's office, and actively listen when they talk to you.

5. Positive Reinforcement

As Ken Blanchard of *One Minute Manager* fame showed, positive reinforcement encourages repeated, desirable performance. This is possibly the simplest part of any communication plan, aside from not getting along with one's boss—without fail, the main reason people change jobs is lack of recognition. Honest praise is better than a raise. Financial incentives are very important, but a pat on the back is often the most effective executive talent retention strategy going.

6. Adaptation

Key performers contribute a lot: education, brainpower, experience, creativity, and energy. They know they will be right more often than they're wrong and need an environment where they can fully use their talents and creativity. The problem is that not everything they try will work. So give them and yourself room to adapt. That's a major key to executive talent retention.

7. Involvement in Decision Making

Top performers need involvement, and typically stay where they have a voice and a responsive ear. With exceptional performers, however, it is mandatory that they be involved in key decision making. If your top performers aren't involved, they're gone. This is true at every level in organizations, so ensure the executives you hire also have the emotional intelligence to lead in this manner as well.

Compensation

A good compensation program holds the final three keys for attracting and keeping the best executives.

In the real world, if the cash side is insufficient, you have no room for error in any other area of retention. Money can be a highly effective lever for prying executives loose. It won't generally be the only or even deciding factor, but it gets them to listen hard to the other components of an offer. As an executive's existing financial package gets better and better, it puts increasing pressure on any new deal to be not only better, but to be outstandingly better in the other areas (challenge, opportunity, visibility, etc.) in order to balance the risk involved in making a change.

8. Exceeding Industry Norms

Few companies choose to exceed the market in base salaries for key executives. Those that do usually also have better-than-industry plans in long-term compensation and bonuses. Long-term incentives tied to KPIs are good for the organization and are concrete measuring sticks for executives. Too Pavlovian? I don't think so. Consider it a continuous course correction factor, like autopilot on a boat. These companies attract high-quality executives who don't want to leave. How do employees rank compensation elements? As motivators to remain, two areas rank high with employees: salary and long-term incentives. Three other areas—short-term incentives, benefits, and perquisites—are moderately important to them.

9. Long-Term Ties

The second component of a good compensation program—the use of long-term financial ties—is perhaps the most important. Make it expensive for executives to leave before you want them to. Incentives must be real and attainable, but you can stagger payouts or associate payouts with loyalty and longevity. Take care, however, to construct a package that's perceived by the executive as a positive incentive rather than restrictive handcuffs.

10. Over-the-Top Rewards

The final component of a good retention package is one that rewards exceptional performance generously. This means performance that significantly exceeds high expectations. Cash, gifts, airline tickets, weekend or week-long getaways, a golf or fishing trip with the boss, an invitation to dinner—all are valued and appropriate rewards that will contribute to a long-term relationship. In my experience, when an executive achieves beyond the norm it's usually a group effort—and the spouse who feels appreciated is less likely to support (or advocate for) a move to a new situation. Make the package first-class and always consider the executive's family and personal life. Do it right, or don't do it at all. (Trust us on this—we've nailed more wingtips to the deck with this strategy than all others combined.)

People don't quit companies—they quit bosses! Thankfully, the only thing you need do to keep headhunters at bay is pretty basic: Keep all the promises you made while courting them, even the ones that weren't documented.

COUNTEROFFERS

Don't even consider it. If it happens, hang your ESP, who should have been discussing the potential of a counteroffer early and often with candidates. By the time the process is finished, the intellectual decision to join has been made. Download the special report on counteroffers at the website.

Counter offer brochure.

CONCLUSION

In the introduction, we stated, "There are very few opportunities for a company to improve organizational performance and culture by taking just one single action. Hiring Greatness is one of them." We compared Marissa Mayer and Ron Johnson because contrasting the two offered such an extreme example of the value of attracting the right executive to the right role—in this case $21.3B. At the time she was hired, Marissa Meyer was the sixth CEO in five years at Yahoo![2] Most companies don't have the luxury of time, nor the money, to keep hiring executives until they get it right. Likewise, Ron Johnson, who had a solid career at Apple and Target, was clearly the wrong fit for JCPenney and shouldn't have been placed in that role.

Those of us involved daily in the management of a business know that every investment must be measured by the returns it produces for all stakeholders in a business. Too often management views the acquisition of staff as a simple process of expansion, but the acquisition of key players is an investment like any other—one that should have a demonstrative return on investment (ROI), and clearly justifies the effort and cost involved.

Mark and I have seen, firsthand, the results of Hiring Greatness at early-stage companies, SMBs, billion-dollar multinationals, and Fortune 500 companies. Our clients expect greatness, and the executives we've hired have achieved some impressive returns for their companies:

- Ignited 700 percent growth and ever-increasing earnings, drove stock from $3.90 to a peak of $68.

- Grew sales from $8M to $77M in six years with more than 29 percent EBITDA, exited with three times multiple.

- Moved last place company (globally) from worst to first and an exit in less than 10 months.

- Sales jumped 497 percent in first 15 months, delivered greater than 30 percent CAGR year over year for five years.

- Resuscitated company, took share price of $0.69 to a high of $7.10, acquired for six times multiple.

- This repositioned company morphed from approximately $440M to $3.2B.

Some journeys are more impactful than others. Hiring Greatness is one of them. Indeed, there are few initiatives as strategically challenging, as demanding on management, and as fundamentally disruptive to normal operations as a leadership search. But at the same time a successful executive search is the only initiative that can so thoroughly move a company to the next level, and to a place it can realize its potential.

Hiring Greatness, when done right, isn't just valuable—it's critical.

Notes

1. www.humanresourcesiq.com/hr-talent-management/articles/executive-talent-retention-how-to-recruiter-proof/.
2. www.wsj.com/articles/SB100014240527023037549045775312305 41447956.

EPILOGUE: ALL IN
Touched by Greatness

There is a very simple reason why I believe in the power of greatness. It's because I was touched by greatness firsthand. It saved—and changed—my life on April 13th, 1971 . . . .

The urgent rhythm of the approaching medical transport helicopter shattered the calm of the thin Colorado air. I always had mixed feelings whenever I heard such helicopters in the night: a foreboding concern for whomever might need that immediate medical attention, partially offset by guilt-ridden relief that at least "it wasn't me."

But this time, it was for me.

Drifting in and out of medicated sedation, I was amused as the bright lights overhead seemed to swirl around the hospital's surgical amphitheater. Over 100 visiting doctors were crammed into the upper surgical observatory. The pre-op support team was bustling with activity, in anticipation of the imminent arrival of the distinguished team of surgeons disembarking from the helicopter.

The military surgeons at Fitzsimons Army Hospital in Denver had been blunt with my father: No one had ever survived the heart operation I was about to undergo. The attending nurse whispered compassionately to my father, "You need to say good-bye now." My dad squeezed my hand and, in a soft tone percolating with hope, he looked into my eyes, smiled bravely, and said, "You'll be alright, Dave. I love you, son," as the cluster of doctors arrived.

My father was assured these doctors were among the greatest team of heart surgeons in the world. That claim was validated when I went through 12 hours of open-heart surgery, and beat the overwhelming odds to survive. Seven months of rehab later and I was back to 100 percent. I've never met the U.S. Army surgical team that performed that miracle on me that day, but there's no question I owe my life to the collective greatness of their divinely guided hands.[1]

Looking back, I was eight years old in 1968 when my family—mother, father, two sisters, and I—moved from Royal Roads Military College in Victoria, British Columbia, to the U.S. Air Force Academy in Colorado Springs, Colorado. We were the only Canadians on the base. Tragedy struck within days of our arrival when my mother, Coleen, suffered a stroke while my parents were attending their very first dinner at the new boss's house.

My mother subsequently spent many months in the hospital and, since my father worked such long hours, my two baby sisters were temporarily sent to live with relatives in Halifax, Nova Scotia. I stayed on the base under the ever-watchful eye of an extended community of caring neighbors. I was in essence "functionally adopted" by several families in our cluster and was welcomed into their homes to eat, sleep, and play.

The genuine concern and collaborative culture of the base remains fondly etched in my memory. People were passionately engaged in trying to build a better world for themselves and others. On weekends, while my father was visiting my mother in the hospital, I gladly participated in community work, joining my "adopted families" in goodwill exploits like painting the school, repairing the church, or helping neighbors with heavy yardwork.

Those gestures—big or small—were sincere, executed with love, and had immense impact on those we assisted. It felt good to be part of that. I witnessed the power of the greatness that was America. I liked it.

In the summer of 1971 my father was posted to Toronto and we returned to Canada. I didn't want to leave. I will forever hold the deepest appreciation for America and the unbridled kindness and genuine care our American friends extended to my entire family. A nation's greatness is distinguished by its compassion, and we certainly felt the full measure of America's greatness.

Eleven years later, in 1982, I graduated with an economics degree from McGill University. After working for several recruiting firms for a few years, I started my own executive search firm, Perry-Martel International, in 1988. Over 1,000 successful searches later, here we are.

It vexes me to see the unprecedented pressures on the American psyche including the bludgeoning national debt, perennial trade deficit, alarming decline in the labor force participation rate, escalating future unfunded liabilities, and increased social welfare costs. The impact on the social and political fabric of the country are apparent. Yes, greatness is once again being summoned from the resourceful imperative embodied in the American spirit of defiance, compassion, and resolve.

It's on.

The current conditions are an insult to tolerance and an unsavory challenge to endure. We need all cylinders firing—or at least more of them. Ignoring the micro/macro influences for the moment, and just focusing on scale, consider that in terms of the number of cylinders firing America can dramatically improve the number of people contributing to the bottom line.

Consider that out of an estimated population of 318 million Americans:

- 61 million *can't work*—under 16, and too young.

- 102 million *don't work*—of working age, but not in the labor force or unemployed.

- 104 million are *not fully engaged* and productive at their jobs (70 percent of the 148 million that *don't work*).

> The greatness of America lies not in being more enlightened than any other nation, but rather in her ability to repair her faults.
> —**Alexis de Tocqueville**

Accordingly, out of 318 million Americans, only 51 million work at or near full capacity: 267 million do not. That's difficult to sustain in any economic climate, let alone an economy already overburdened by the mammoth challenges already mentioned.

In the years since we left Colorado, my affinity and admiration for America has never wavered. Nor has my belief in her capacity for greatness. America has accomplished many great things in its illustrious history. I'll forego trite recaps of such triumphs, and instead say I think it's imperative for the country's exceptional leadership to undertake what must be done now and in the future. Cliché as it sounds, the need for greatness has never been more pronounced in America and, indeed, throughout the world.

My concern for America's well being is sincere, as is my belief in her ability to meet the challenges confronting her. Alexis de Tocqueville said "The greatness of America lies not in being more enlightened than any other nation, but rather in her ability to repair her faults." So be it.

— David Perry

P.S. What really impressed me more than landing a man on the moon—was bringing him back!

NOTE

1. Fitzimmons General Army Hospital, Denver, Colorado. The cardiac surgery department staff (at the time): Majors Wheeling and Brott, surgeons, and Lt. Colonel Strevey, Assistant Chief of Thoracic-Cardiovascular Service

ACKNOWLEDGMENTS

No man is an iland, intire of it selfe; every man is a peece of the Continent, a part of the maine; if a clod bee washed away by the Sea, Europe is the lesse, as well as if a Promontorie were, as well as if a Mannor of thy friends or of thine owne were; any mans death diminishes me, because I am involved in Mankinde; And therefore never send to know for whom the bell tolls; It tolls for thee . . . .

—John Donne, Meditation 17, Devotions
upon Emergent Occasions (1674)

The same holds true in 2016 as it did back in the year 1674 when this passage was originally put to paper. In the case of *Hiring Greatness* with two authors, it was not one man nor was it two men who ultimately helped shape this book.

Our team at Wiley continuously amaze me with their patience, kindness, and raw intellect. Shannon, Liz, Peter, and Abirami are a force of nature within the publishing industry. It has been David's good fortune to have worked with them for many years.

Many other people lent their expertise as well, and without their help it would not have been possible for this book to be in your hands. Therefore our underlying gratitude goes to Fred Teshinsky, Jim Rulseh, Carl Albert, Peter Dubois, Jim Donnelly, Janette Levey Frisch, Esq., Rayanne Thorn, Joe Zinner, and Heather Bussing.

Insight into the profession of executive search and recruiting has been scarce and much of what the authors have learned comes from other disciplines beyond HR. As such there are giants in the business whose influence we would like to recognize: A. Robert Taylor, John Tarrant, Peter Leffkowitz, Bill Vick, Tony Bruno, Steven M. Finkel, and David's first mentor Robert (Bob) Heanault.

The authors would also like to thank the thousands of clients and candidates with whom we have worked through the years for allowing us to help make their companies and their careers a success, which in turn has allowed the authors to not only grow professionally, but personally as well and in turn enjoy the lifestyles we have worked so hard and so long to achieve.   _____

Position Profile

EXECUTIVE SEARCH MANDATE

Chief Operating Officer

Confidential Search

An established and very profitable manufacturing company with over 200 employees in three locations across North America is seeking an experienced business leader with an engineering or manufacturing background to lead its business, to leverage the company's unique IP and manufacturing capabilities, to extend its current product lines, and to develop profitable new additions to its current offerings.

The company today has several large customers in both the injection molding and capital goods manufacturing markets. The injection molding customers manufacture products utilized in industrial and consumer applications. The company enjoys long and successful relationships in this area and utilizes its patented processes to allow manufacturing of uniquely profitable, high quality components for these applications. The company also has a capital goods manufacturing business focused on manufacturing equipment for construction and capital equipment used in several industries. Some of the equipment is used in defense applications. The company's injection molding business is based primarily in Wisconsin and New York State, and its capital goods business is on the West Coast.

The company has a 35-year track record of profitable operations and has expanded and diversified through both acquisitions and organic growth. By drawing on engineering and manufacturing strengths, in an entrepreneurial and opportunistic culture, the company has constantly innovated new products and manufacturing methods, leveraging the expertise and infrastructure of the company while fulfilling key customer needs and producing very profitable results. Clients view the company as a key strategic supplier and partner. The company treats key clients as "partners," developing a key position in the supply chain of the clients.

The Company

The company has developed valuable manufacturing and engineering expertise over the last 35-plus years of profitable operations and has been a key partner to its manufacturing and construction customers. Its products are utilized across a broad range of industries and across the globe. It has a well-established reputation for innovation and for customer service. It prides itself in responsiveness and flexibility as its customers' needs develop, grow, and change. It builds considerable inventory to allow for fluctuations in demand while maintaining predictable on-time delivery performance.

To maintain product quality and to support its ongoing renewal process, the company devotes significant resources to fabrication of molds of many sizes and complexities. It has complete facilities to perform materials analysis and manufacturing process refinement. It has tools for mold flow analysis and robotic assembly. It utilizes SPC on its high-volume operations and is ISO9000 compliant in its Wisconsin- and New York State–based operations.

The company's challenge is to refine and extend its current high quality product offerings, deepen its key customer relationships in its served industries including automotive, lawn and garden equipment, defense, beverage containers, and waste recycling while concurrently exploring new profitable product offerings to leverage the intellectual and physical assets of the company.

This is a challenging position. The company is highly profitable, not a "turnaround" situation. Your job is to continue to improve this profitability by developing new opportunities and expanding existing lines of business. The company uses well-developed metrics for management. The owner/CEO is a smart, creative, entrepreneurial, tough, and very competent manager. He knows when to say no to requests for capital investment and when to say yes to requests that will enhance the business. He knows when to cut staff to meet economic contraction conditions and when to add people to meet expansion opportunities. The company is looking for a person with the same talents and capabilities. Are you ready for this kind of a challenge?

The Opportunity

We are seeking a senior individual with a solid understanding of general business, a strong background in manufacturing and engineering, a demonstrated ability to lead a manufacturing business and leverage a company's assets to grow and adapt to dynamic market conditions. The individual must have personally led the design and/or manufacture of both high volume components and capital goods. The individual must understand how to profitably manage a mature manufacturing and service-centric business while personally developing and strengthening relationships to grow the company.

Our ideal candidate is bright with a tremendous innate curiosity and a thirst for understanding. The candidate must thrive in both extreme detail and high-level abstraction. The candidate must have a complete understanding of all aspects of manufacturing including order entry, materials forecasting, process engineering, product engineering, and quality manufacturing practices. The candidate must have experience managing suppliers, introducing new products, and providing leadership to drive profitable performance and reliable products and delivery performance. The person for this position will be equally comfortable on the manufacturing floor and in the boardroom and is a natural communicator.

You will be responsible for leading all aspects of manufacturing, product engineering, and client satisfaction. You will be based in Wisconsin and will focus on supporting current customers and maintaining and improving profitability. You will constantly seek to deliver compelling new products and draw freely on a talented staff and the CEO to evaluate product enhancements and extensions. You will participate in meetings of the board of directors.

You will:

- Develop a deep understanding of the company's manufacturing operations and sustainable distinctions.

- Quickly gain the respect and loyalty of the staff and work with the CEO to agree on the key performance metrics to be measured and improved.

- Develop a rapport with key customers and understand the role we play in their success.

- Develop and maintain executive-level relationships with all suppliers and customers.

- Provide a constant focus on careful spending and waste reduction. Lead continuous process improvement initiatives.

- Prepare and present proposals to both partners and partner prospects.

- Drive product innovation and assure maximum leverage of current infrastructure, core competencies, and experience.

- Provide financial oversight on operations; initially focus on the injection molding business and then the capital goods manufacturing and metal-forming business.

- Brief the CEO and the board on manufacturing, financial performance, product development, customer support, and quality improvements.

- Travel to all company locations to lead unified operations initiatives and provide a corporate context for each operation's activities.

Your Background

You are a senior business professional. You recognize and enjoy the need to push yourself to identify the "next big thing." You thrive on your accomplishments and cannot accept merely being adequate. You have proven success leading a manufacturing company. You are proud of the improvements you have made, the ingenuity you've demonstrated, the organizations you've led, and the people you've recruited to work with you. You enjoy your work.

You have a positive attitude and a high energy level. You are bright, curious, and always anxious to learn and self-improve. You are flexible and can change approach and/or direction as may be required. You have exceptional interpersonal skills and have strong verbal presentation abilities. You have a professional business demeanor and are skilled in bringing concepts, services, and quality products to the marketplace. You exhibit a take-charge attitude, persistence, tenacity, and drive focused on finding a way to accomplish your objectives. You influence others with your drive and sense of urgency, and possess the highest level of integrity.

Your peers would describe you as "an enthusiastic and extremely disciplined team player who will work to achieve the goals of the firm via a team orientation, detailed involvement, and strong personal contribution." You are seeking an opportunity to grow an exceptionally profitable company and extend its capabilities into new markets and opportunities.

Ideally you have:

- Experience and skills pertaining to the management of both capital goods and component manufacturing business models.

- Experience in growing mature products to new levels of financial performance.

- Exceptional track record working with existing customers and with development of new business prospects.

- Personal product innovation and process improvement skills.

- Demonstrated experience leading cross-functional teams to drive improved margins.

- Broad-based manufacturing and engineering knowledge with experience in materials characterization and statistical process control.

- Candidates having experience with plastics or metal-forming operations strongly preferred.

- 15 to 20 years of profitable business management experience.

Compensation

The working environment and culture of this company is unique and offers an outstanding opportunity for the right senior executive. The company offers a highly competitive compensation package.

Your Next Step

All inquiries and discussions are strictly confidential. Contact David Perry at 613-236-6995 or e-mail dperry@perrymartel.com or Mark Haluska at haluska@comcast.net. For more information on Perry-Martel International Inc. please visit our website at www .perrymartel.com

Confidential Candidate Brief

WORKING WITH PERRY-MARTEL INTERNATIONAL INC.

Confidential Candidate Brief for Manufacturing COO

The purpose of this Brief is to gather preliminary information and then to match **your** requirements with the needs of our client regarding the above position. This document is a critical part of the selection and preparation process.

When you're finished please save the document with ["your name" Confidential Brief] and then submit the completed brief to: dperry@perrymartel.com or haluska@comcast.net

At this early stage in the process, do understand that we take your candidacy very seriously; that is why this has been sent to you. Please recognize though, that Perry-Martel cannot make *any* guarantee that you will be granted an interview or a job offer for the above position.

Kindly address *all* of the following questions. In preparing for your job search you probably have most of the information at your fingertips already. We think you'll agree that your next career move is worth the thoughtful effort. Please avoid the use of terms such as "see résumé" or other such phrases. It is important that you think through and verbalize your answers to prepare you for any subsequent interview process.

Also be sure you include your updated Microsoft Word résumé, as a separate attachment, in support of this document. Please visit our website for more information that may be helpful to your career: www .perrymartel.com.

Thank you,

David Perry and Mark J. Haluska

You can use the "Page Up" and "Page Down" keys to navigate back and forth on this document.

1. Your name:

2. Today's date:

3. Phone number(s):   Home:

4. Cell: (Optional)

5. Personal e-mail:

6. Generally speaking, when is the best time to contact you? (Include time zone)

7. Are you currently employed? Yes ☐ No ☐

8. Your current/last job title:

9. Dates (month/year) employed at this title:

10. Current /last employer company name:

11. If you are currently unemployed, please explain the circumstances that led to this status?
☐ Not applicable. I am still employed as of this date.
I left my last position because

12. If necessary, are you willing to relocate to Wisconsin?
☐ Yes ☐ No

13. This position requires engineering, manufacturing, and business management skills. Can you take a moment and tell me where you have had these responsibilities. What products did you build and with what results (market share, revenues, and profit margins)?
Comments:

14. Tell me about your experience with analyzing and interpreting financial data. Are you confident in your ability to read, analyze, and interpret income statements and balance sheets? Give an example of the insight you have gained and decisive action taken from analyzing financial information.
Comments:

15. How would you best describe your personal management/leadership style? Explain how your style is perceived by your boss, peers, and subordinates. What would you do to improve your management acumen?
Comments:

16. What is your direct experience with suppliers and OEM customers in developing new products? Explain how your prior experience is relevant to building these relationships. Are any of these defense customers?
Comments:

17. Cite examples of experience you have in dealing with large capital goods manufacturing customers, specifically in support of their core product lines? Identify your strongest success and greatest frustration in these engagements.
Comments:

18. Where have you demonstrated the ability to successfully manage a mature business or product line to maximize profitability? Describe initiatives you took to minimize cost, retain customers, improve service, and improve profitability.
Comments:

19. Give an example of an innovative approach you have taken to respond quickly to an unanticipated resource demand. Further, explain how quality (of products and services delivered) and the volume of sales was impacted by those actions.
Comments:

20. Describe your experience in communications with or participating on company boards of directors. Have you ever led the process of acquisition or restructuring?
    Comments:

21. How have you developed and deployed new products that leverage existing manufacturing infrastructure and core competencies? Have you ever personally led both the development and the interactions with early adopter customers? Please elaborate.
    Comments:

22. Describe what you believe to be your two most recent major professional accomplishments *relative to the position profile for COO.* How do these reflect your personal learning and growth in these efforts?
    Comments:

23. This is a position that requires a senior player/coach capable of both strategic and multilevel operational management. Have you demonstrated these skills in the past, and if so, how?
    ☐ No ☐ Yes
    Comments:

24. Under what circumstances would you accept a counteroffer from your current employer?
    ☐ Not applicable as I am currently unemployed.
    ☐ I would not accept a counteroffer for any reason.
    I might consider a counteroffer from my employer if:

25. What is the primary reason you would like to confidentially explore this opportunity?
    Comments:

26. Are you currently working under an unexpired employment contract?
    ☐ Yes ☐ No
    Comments:

27. Have you signed any non-disclosure agreements or non-compete agreements that are still in effect?

    ☐ No ☐ Yes

    If yes, please explain:

28. Degrees attained, certifications, patents granted, continuing education, professional affiliations, and so on are an important indicator of your breadth of experience and thirst for knowledge. Please take a moment to list any degrees, certifications, or other designations and the year they were granted.

    Comments:

29. As always, there is a legal question. Your confidentiality is an important matter. Perry-Martel International maintains candidate data in a **privately owned and secure** database. Do we have permission to store your information in our database?

    ☐ Yes ☐ No

30. This brief is a tool that we first use to help us determine your suitability relative to the needs of our client. If referred to our client, this brief may also be utilized in their internal evaluation process. May we provide our client with the information contained in this document?

    ☐ Yes ☐ No

    Comments:

Thank you for taking time to address the confidential candidate brief. We are now better positioned to confidentially and intelligently speak with you about this opportunity and to present your credentials.

INDEX

Printed in the USA/Agawam, MA
September 19, 2022

798746.021